BIRDS
of
THAILAND

BIRDS
of
THAILAND

Text and photographs
Roland Eve
Anne-Marie Guigue

Illustrations
Roland Eve

Translation
Patricia Arnold

TIMES EDITIONS

Birds of Thailand
© **1996 Times Editions Pte Ltd**

First published in French in 1995 by
Times Editions Pte Ltd
Times Centre, 1 New Industrial Road
Singapore 536196

Times Subang
Lot 46, Subang Hi-Tech Industrial Park
Batu Tiga
40000 Shah Alam
Selangor Darul Ehsan, Malaysia

Printed in Malaysia

ISBN: 981-204-780-8

Summary

Foreword

This book makes no claim to be either an ornithological or a travel guide. Instead, it is an invitation to discover and an incentive to look at and understand the bird life of Thailand.

We wished to evoke the environment in which there are more than 920 species of birds and to describe some aspects of their biology. Then to get a little closer to 123 species with a description of their way of life. In choosing among those closest to humans, the most visible as well as the most typical of the principal species of Indochina, we wanted to show the astonishing wealth of shapes, colours and behaviours of the birds of this country. Our choice of species did not follow a strict or reasoned approach but rather followed our affinity with certain groups of birds, particularly those living in the forest.

In order to supplement a partial and rather personal choice we have added, at the end, an exhaustive list of birds of Thailand, showing whether they are residents or visitors, so that the reader may refer to it for information on those species not mentioned in the main part of the book.

Acknowledgements

We should first like to pay tribute to the great ornithologist and pioneer of nature conservation in his country, Dr. Boonsong Lekagul, who died in 1992, and for the hours spent in his company in the shadowy light of his large office, its walls covered with trophies, shelves full of strange objects, books and specimens.

This book is dedicated in particular to the staff working for the protection of nature in Thailand, who have the responsibility of saving and passing on millions of years of living heritage. Continuous logistical support for the Royal Forest Department allowed us to carry out numerous field studies. We should like to thank all those in charge of the parks and reserves who welcomed us so generously, in particular Messrs Jira Jintanugool, Noporat Naksatit and Panya Preedeesanit.

Special mention is due to Christopher and Sandra Hails whose friendship and hospitality were greatly appreciated during our visits to Asia.

Roland Eve would like to thank his first field companions in Thailand, David Melville and Philip Round, for their friendship and knowledge, as well as Dr. David Wells whose advice he has benefitted from throughout these years.

Jean-Pascal Beaufils, Agnes Guigue and Marie-Christine Vellozzi aided us with comments and suggestions on the text. Jean-Pascal Beaufils also drew the map of Thailand.

Pierre Le Marechal kindly provided us with the French ornithologist nomenclature (for the French edition) which was a tremendous help.

The collections of bird specimens in Bangkok and Paris were studied and photographed thanks to the kind permission of Dr. Niphan Ratanaworobhan, Director of the Ecological Section of the Thailand Institute of Scientific and Technological Research for the National Reference Collection, and Professor Christian Erard, Director of the Mammal and Bird Laboratory at the National History Museum in Paris.

Finally our thanks go to our parents and to our friends in France and Southeast Asia who, each in his own way, encouraged and supported us during the preparation of this book.

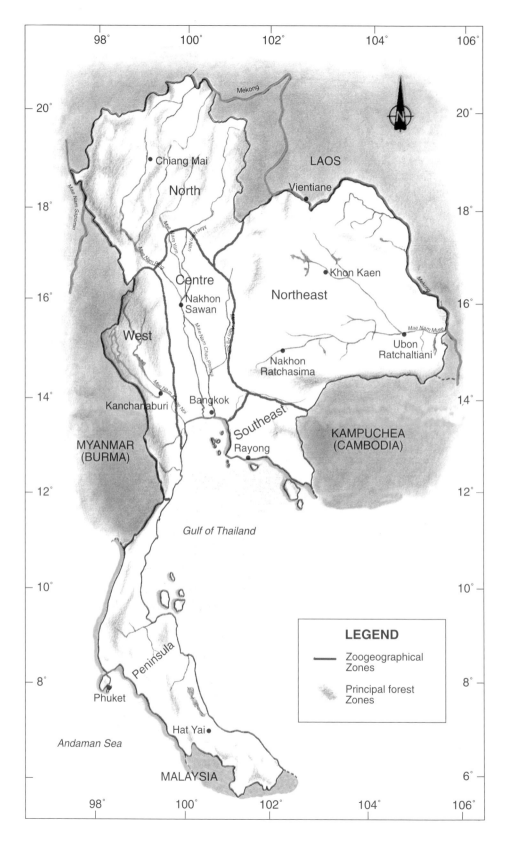

Introduction to the Country

Thailand has become a popular tourist destination, shown in tourist brochures as smiling, exotic and sometimes torrid. It is still unusual for any mention to be made of its rich natural heritage. This country, nevertheless, harbours an extraordinary diversity of vegetable and animal life. More than 920 species of birds have been identified, of which approximately two thirds are resident and one third migratory.

With a total surface area of 513,115 square kilometres, Thailand stretches over 1,600 kilometres from north to south and has 2,600 kilometres of coastline. To that can be added several hundred islands scattered in the Gulf of Thailand and the Andaman Sea. The mainland region takes up 84% of the surface area of the country, which extends southwards as a peninsula, demarcated by the Isthmus of Kra at Prachuap Kiri Kan (11°4′ north).

The tropical climate is characterised by three seasons: a dry and cool season from November to February, brought by the northeast continental monsoon; a hot season from March to May; and the rainy season brought on by the southwest monsoon from the Andaman Sea. September is usually the wettest month. In the southeast of the peninsula the rains can continue from November to January.

The average national rainfall is between 1,100 and 1,550 millimetres a year, but the distribution over the country is uneven. Some regions of the peninsula and the southeast receive more than 3,000 millimetres (4,300 mms at Ranong and Klong Yai), whereas Kanchanaburi in the southwest gets only 994 millimetres of rain.

Temperatures vary depending on region and altitude, the annual national average being about 27°C in the plain. Temperatures are relatively stable in the peninsula and coastal regions, inland the differences are more pronounced. The coolest period is December to January, with an average minimum temperature of 10°C. April is the hottest month with record temperatures of nearly 40°C.

THE NATURAL ENVIRONMENT

Human presence in Southeast Asia is ancient in origin, but for a long time the population was widely dispersed and had little impact on the natural environment. It is only recently that rapid changes have occurred in the environment.

Originally Thailand was covered by forest and savannah. As time passed humans settled there, shaping the countryside to suit their needs. The first systematic changes began in the Neolithic period when humans began practicing agriculture and domesticating animals. Subsequently, there was a succession of powerful kingdoms in the fertile deltas along the rivers. Sukhothai, Khmer, Mon and Ayuthaya knew grandeur and decadence. They left their mark on the countryside and the ruins of their cities in a region which was to become the Kingdom of Siam, and in 1939, Thailand.

Thanks to irrigation methods, rice became the staple food, while commercial activities, such as forestry and mining developed progressively. The modernization of the country intensified after World War II, bringing strong economic growth. Meanwhile, the population grew from 8 million in 1910 to more than 55 million today.

Population growth has had a major impact on the environment, reflected here, as everywhere else, in a reduction in natural resources and biodiversity. Before World War II, 70% of the country was covered by primary forest. Today less than 15% of the forest remains intact, often restricted to hilly terrain.

Cultivated areas have increased considerably, particularly in the flat lands where mechanisation has been aided by the absence of hills. Food producing culture has been replaced by intensive agriculture or monoculture, rice in the central plain, manioc in the east, and palm oil and rubber in the peninsula.

Large areas have been decimated by ill-considered forestry exploitation with no management policy or suitable reforestation programmes. Following a tragic landslide, claiming several hundred lives in Nakhon Si Thammarat, an upsurge of public feeling resulted in new legislation. Since 1989, the Thai government has officially revoked all forestry concessions, putting a stop to this kind of large-scale deforestation. But the problems have simply shifted to the bordering countries, Burma, Laos, Cambodia.

At the same time, landless peasants have moved in and installed themselves by using the paths opened by the forestry companies. From north to south, these impoverished agriculturists have contributed to tree clearing and also bear responsibility for destruction of forest resources.

From time immemorial the rural population has hunted and gathered produce in the forest, but the impact on the forest remained negligible. Today, with the proliferation of guns and easy access to the forest, the demand for meat, trophies and animal skins has led to a decline in large mammal populations, and the endangerment of remaining animals taking refuge in protected areas.

In a country of rapid economic growth, the development of infrastructure and anarchic urbanisation constitute the

Pine forest in the National Park of Nam Nao in the northeast.

12

most immediate risks to the countryside and the areas still protected.

However, under the Forestry Department, Thailand has established about a hundred parks and nature reserves and is attempting to carry out a concerted policy of nature conservation. The total protected area represents about 9% of Thai territory. Human and material resources are sometimes still inadequate for the task, but this system of conservation is the only guarantee of biological diversity in this part of the world.

ZOOGEOGRAPHICAL REGIONS

Situated in the heart of the Indochinese peninsula, Thailand benefits from biogeographical influences that have contributed to the enrichment of its natural heritage with species of Himalayan and Chinese origin in the mountains of the north, Indochinese in the eastern part of the country, Malayan in the peninsula, and Indian and Burmese in the west. The distribution of these different species, especially the birds, has allowed naturalists to define six Thai zoogeographical zones.

The Centre

The central region is formed by a great alluvial plain which stretches on each side of the River Menam (Chao Phraya) and reaches to its mouth in the Gulf of Thailand. The main rice-growing area of the country, it is also, along with Bangkok and its suburbs, the most urban.

This vast marshy area was the home of colonies of storks, herons, ibis, cranes and pelicans, and the refuge of vultures, eagles and kites. Today these colonies have decreased greatly or disappeared, with the exception of the more ecologically adaptable species that took refuge in various sanctuaries.

The North

Situated between the Salween and

Mekong rivers, the northern region is mainly mountainous, the continuation of the Tibetan-Himalayan massif, with summits often rising over 1,500 metres. The highest point, Doi Inthanon, is 2,590 metres. The serious deforestation on the plain and in the foothills is attributable to the mountain tribes who slash and burn to improve the soil and assure themselves survival. The most numerous species of mountain birds, whether residents or migrants, are found in this region.

The Northeast

Formed by the dry and relatively low Plateau of Korat, surrounded by the mountain ranges of Dangrek, Khao Khieng, the Dong Phya Yen and the valley of the Mekong river, the northeastern region, with a high population density, is largely agricultural. There are several protected forest areas, such as the national parks of Khao Yai and Nam Nao, which shelter a wealth of wildlife.

The Southeast

The southeastern region, bordering Cambodia, is the smallest of the zoogeographical zones. Open to the Gulf of Thailand, it is largely an area of plains, bordered in the north by the remote mountains of Khao Soi Dao. Several Indochinese species and sub-species similar to those found in the forest in the south of Cambodia and Vietnam, occur there.

The West

The western region borders the Burmese frontier and the mountainous folds extend as far as the Isthmus of Kra. It forms a fairly continuous area of forest between the north and the south.

Vast deciduous and dry evergreen forests have been preserved, particularly in the reserves of Huai Kha Kaeng and Thung Yai, now registered with World Heritage. It is here that most of the large mammals of Asia still survive, as well as some rare birds, such as the Green Peafowl and White-Winged Duck.

The Peninsula

Starting at latitude 11°40' north, the peninsula appears as a mosaic of plains and fractured mountain massifs. The highest point, Khao Lung, rises to 1,835 metres. The rain forest which once covered the whole area is now mainly confined to the hill slopes.

The bird population differs from that in the rest of Thailand, consisting mainly of Sundaic species similar to those found in the rain forests of Malaysia and Indonesia.

TWO ENDEMIC SPECIES

A region of plains and plateaux open to free genetic flows, Thailand was not a sanctuary for new forms of animals during the Ice Age. As a result it harbours few endemic species, that is to say birds found only within its frontiers. Only two have been spotted: the White-eyed River Martin (*Pseudochelidon sirintarae*) and the Deignan's Babbler (*Stachyris rodolphei*).

The history of the White-eyed River Martin is quite remarkable. Nine of these small black birds, shaped like swallows, were captured by chance in 1968 on the Lake of Bung Borapet (in

Nakhon Sawan province). Since then, this mysterious species, unknown elsewhere, has only been seen three times, always in the company of large groups of swallows. Nothing is known of its ecology other than that the rare sightings have each time been between November and February, indicating that Lake Bung Borapet is a wintering site. Can one assume that the bird nests in China? An illustration of a bird made in China in about 1970 and found recently is very similar to the White-eyed River Martin and has revived the mystery of its origin.

Although very rare, the Deignan's Babbler is less mysterious. This bird of the undergrowth is in fact restricted to the bamboo forests of the mountains of Doi Chiang Dao, near Chiang Mai. It was found and described by Herbert Deignan, the first ornithologist to produce a complete list of the birds of Thailand in 1963.

Woodpeckers' nests in a pine trunk.

There are other endemic species which are also limited to a small geographical area straddling several frontiers. For example, the Siamese Fireback, a pheasant which lives only in Thailand and Indochina; the Chestnut-headed Partridge, found only in the evergreen forests in the hills of southeast Thailand and southwest Cambodia; and the Limestone Wren-Babbler, whose preference is for the limestone crags in a zone between Tenasserim and northern Vietnam.

The recent discovery of Gurny's Pitta in 1986 and the research undertaken before is a good illustration of the problems associated with endemism. This magnificent multi-coloured bird lives only in the rain forest on the plain of the Thai peninsula and the extreme south of Tenasserim in Burma.

Lack of sightings in the field after 1952 and the almost complete destruction of its habitat suggested that it might have disappeared. But after four years of research, individuals were discovered in the Bangkok bird market. Discussions with local trappers led to the sighting of a nesting couple in a forest near Krabi. Other couples were then discovered in bordering regions. The media interest which this discovery provoked soon led to protective measures for the site and a programme on conservation education for the villagers. Some trappers were even promoted to wardens in the nature reserve!

The Birds

For most of us the discovery of birds occurs gradually. It starts with identification, that is to say, the ability to name a bird. The bird then filters into the field of knowledge of the observer and thus acquires an existence. Subsequently, each identified species becomes associated with the image of a region, a countryside, a moment in the day or a season. This association between a bird and a place, geographical location and time, introduces notions of ecology, ethnology (science of animal behaviour) and biological rhythms which constitute, with a number of other elements of animal and vegetable life, natural history.

In this book, each bird has two names: the vernacular (Sooty-headed Bulbul) and the scientific name, which by convention is written in italics (*Pyconotus aurigaster*). The first term, *Pyconotus*, refers to the genus (a classification grouping families). The second, *aurigaster*, defines the species. Sometimes a third term, defining sub-species, has been added to the text.

A Striped-chested Bulbul (Pycnonotus squamatus) lives in the shaded forests of the peninsula.

Sub-species show slight 'regional' variations in size or plumage, but unlike individuals belonging to distinct species, sub-species interbreed and produce fertile progeny. Today, progress in genetics allows the use of descriptions other than those based on morphology.

There are a certain number of factors in naming and identifying a bird: size, shape, colour, song, behaviour, environment and the region in which it is found.

SIZE AND SHAPE

The first factor is size, a simple feature which allows birdwatchers to distinguish between large and small birds, and offers a point of comparison with those species they are already familiar with (in this book, size is given in centimetres and is measured from the tip of the bill to the tip of the tail). The shape completes the introduction to identification. To determine shape, the different parts of the body are studied, for example the shape and size of the beak, the length of the neck, the feet and the appearance of the tail and the wings. These morphological elements help in the identification of a large number of birds and provide information on their lifestyle and behaviour. The webbed feet and waterproof plumage of a duck are an adaptation to its aquatic life. The small size and curved beak of the sunbird enable it to hang from and feed from the corolla of flowers, allowing it to draw the nectar from inside the deep corolla. Apart from the major anatomical differences, other more subtle characteristics separate species.

PLUMAGE AND COLOURS

Detailed examination of the colour of the plumage often constitutes the first step in identification. The colours, as such, do not exist. They appear as luminous waves and disappear in the absence of light. The surface of the feathers of a red bird, for example, has a molecular composition which absorbs all light radiation with the exception of red. The feathers themselves are colourless and the physico-chemico colour effect we see depends solely on the source of light. This illustrates how the perception of colour can be subjective and variable according to the amount of light available. Therefore, to identify a bird, knowledge of colours should always be accompanied by morphological observations.

Tropical birds are far more brilliantly coloured than those of temperate regions. Various hypotheses have been advanced to explain this difference: the presence of an abundance of food throughout the year favours a high metabolism, allowing the production of a sometimes exuberant plumage; some 'luxury' feathers have a feeble calorific power which only allows them to appear in hot climates; the abundant richness of animal species in the tropics necessitates diversity in external characteristics.

The pattern of colours on the plumage is an invaluable aid in the identification of species. It can also aid in the recognition of sexes and the different stages of life (juvenile, immature, adult). Colour can vary depending on sex (the male often being more brightly coloured), age (a juvenile bird can go through several separate phases before acquiring its adult plumage), and season (male plumage being brighter during than after the breeding season).

The bright and often strongly contrasting marks are part of a system of visual communication between birds. They also help synchronise flight patterns and other activities of birds in close proximity. Certain behaviours or attitudes accentuate the marks or contrast in plumage. For instance, white spots (or contrasting ones) marking the wings or rump appear when the birds take flight, announcing take off and helping to synchronise movements between individuals, such as the Blue-winged Pitta and the Dollarbird. The Black-headed Woodpecker keeps its wings folded along its body rather than crossed on its back on reaching a tree trunk, making the bright red brilliance of its rump very visible which acts as a signal

Like all Kingfishers, the White-throated Kingfisher of Smyrne shows strong iridescent coloration.

to other birds.

Courtship displays, which take place during the nesting period, are a form of demonstration and exhibition of plumage, as much with the object of attracting females as keeping other males away. This phenomenon is particularly spectacular in the Green Peafowl which displays its long dazzling feathers in the form of a wheel in front of the female. Conversely, dull plumage helps to camouflage the bird with its surroundings. The mimetic plumage of nocturnal birds, such as owls, nightjars and frogmouths (the most procryptically successful birds) makes them almost invisible in the countryside especially when they are quite still, with eyelids closed.

Moulting

In order to maintain and conserve the calorific, waterproofing and flying qualities of their feathers, birds renew their plumage by moulting. Hormonal changes in the bird's system cause new feathers to replace worn out ones. Birds generally complete at least one moult a year. Moulting occurs for flight feathers immediately after the breeding season. The other feathers are replaced at different stages throughout the seasons. Moulting involves an important consumption of energy, which for some time afterward affects the birds's capacity for movement. Loss and replacement of feathers follows a strict sequence, and occurs during a period of abundant food reserves.

Swifts and swallows, which feed on the wing and therefore need to be able to fly at all times, replace one feather at a time.

Some species have partial moults during the year. The most remarkable moult occurs just before the breeding season when coloured or ornamental feathers of a sexual nature replace or are added to the plumage. At this time, the tail of the male Common Tailorbird grows by a few centimetres. Egrets grow extra ornamental plumes while the Cattle Egret acquires a red colour on its head and breast. The male Asian Golden Weaver is decorated with bright yellow plumage, which it loses after the breeding season, becoming similar to the female again.

VOICE

Recognition of calls and songs permits the birdwatcher to immediately identify the bird when it is hidden from view. An essential element in the life of a bird, voice works as a remarkable system of communication over distance. It is also an essential function in keeping different individuals in contact for reasons of social cohesion, mating and establishing territorial rights. Each species has a varied repertoire, composed of anywhere from 3 or 4 signals to 15, or sometimes more.

The call is a simple emission of a few notes of one or two syllables. The song is more complex—it is composed of syllables or notes which form a longer phrase. In principle, song is restricted to Oscines and its function is linked to reproduction, contributing to the formation of couples and the establishment of territory. In practice, calls and song are very often mingled, a succession of calls sometimes composing a song.

The male Barred Cuckoo-Dove during courtship.

Call ensures social cohesion within a family or group by signalling the presence of food or the cry of a hungry fledgling. It also allows for the diffusion of information relating to the environment amongst groups of birds, for example, a cry of alarm made at the approach of a predator. Call can also play a role in establishing territory. The volume of sound emitted by the contact calls of the Rufescent Prinia not only keeps the group in contact when moving, but also enables each family to demarcate its food search area.

Other non-vocal noises also act as a form of communication, like the drumming of woodpeckers on tree trunks or the wing clapping of the Red Junglefowl and pigeons.

The different types of sound signals are therefore associated with particular activities and each possesses its own meaning. As such, they are only noticeable at distinct times of the day or year. Early in the morning a veritable chorus can be heard and nearly all the species present can be distinguished. The voices diminish in the middle of the day only to start up again gently late in the afternoon. Nocturnal species are very active vocally at dawn and dusk but less so in the middle of the night.

The breeding season is a good time to hear the range of variations of bird sounds. Vocalisations that appear discordant are, in reality, arranged in space and time so as to enable information to be transmitted in the easiest way possible. Genealogical evolution, the physical constraints of the environment and co-existence with other living creatures also using sound communication (mammals, insects, reptiles) are some of the elements which have contributed to refining this system of communication.

RELATIONS BETWEEN SPECIES

One of the most striking aspects of birdwatching in tropical forests is witnessing the gatherings of large numbers of different species. This could range from a gathering in a tree full of fruit or a 'circling' of insectivores flying through the forest.

Trees laden with ripe fruit attract various species (fig trees are particularly sought after) which assemble and feed at different times of the day. Typically fruit eating birds, such as pigeons, barbets, hornbills and parakeets can be seen and, more sporadically, others with a mixed diet, like bulbuls, flowerpeckers or the Asian Fairy-Bluebird. These feeding groups do not constitute constant and structured social relations, but nevertheless lead to interaction between species, notably in locating fruit trees and in collective vigilance against predators. On the ground, fallen fruit provides a feast for ground birds and mammals.

Social contact takes on another meaning with the forest sparrows which group together to look for food. The collective circling movements allow the birds to flush out the insects camouflaged amongst the foliage.

Flocks gather more commonly during the morning and in the midafternoon. They also gather frequently at the end of the breeding season and throughout the rainy season. The young, barely out of their nests, join the flocks of adults and fly with them long before they can hunt for themselves. During the period of immaturity, whilst flocking with other species, parents feed their young and teach them to collect food for themselves. This period of apprenticeship in the company of other species is one possible explanation for the mutual attraction which unites the birds of these forests.

NESTING SEASONS

In the temperate and northern zones the nesting period occurs when the abundance of spring and summer succeeds the harshness of winter. In the tropics, the climate is more stable but nesting is still seasonal and, as in the temperate zones, coincides with the greater availability of food. This convergence between the breeding and the productive seasons allows the birds to compensate for the large consumption of energy required for the process of reproduction—display, song, territorial defence, nest building, egg production, hatching and feeding the young.

This seasonal pattern is logical in the regions of Thailand where the dry and rainy seasons alternate, the dry season, corresponding to a poor vegetation, comparable to the winter period in temperate zones. More surprising is the similar seasonal reproductive pattern in equatorial areas (in the extreme south of Thailand) where the climate and the amount of daylight are constant throughout the year. There, too, studies show that nesting takes place during periods when there is an abundance of food available.

Most birds nest between February and June, with peak activity in March and April. This period coincides with the end of the dry season and the beginning of the rainy one, which means, for deciduous trees as well as ground vegetation, the regeneration of leaves and grasses. This renewal of vegetation brings to mind the springtime metamorphosis in the more northern countries. The rising sap and the appearance of new leaves is accompanied by the emergence of insects, the most remarkable of which are the cicadas with their concert of chirring sounds. These are consumed by various species of birds, from raptors and leafbirds, to warblers and barbets.

For other types of forest birds, like the pittas, which live in the lower levels of the forest and are ground feeders, nesting takes place in the rainy season of June to October, when the leafmould is crumbly and full of small animals. The water birds, whose survival depends on the availability of water, also nest in the rainy season right up to January. The few species which breed all year round are generally those which nest close to human settlements.

Clutch sizes are smaller in the tropics than in temperate zones, usually two to three eggs for the passerines as opposed to an average of five for their counterparts in temperate zones.

Opposite, a nesting colony of Openbills.

This low rate of reproduction is compensated by a longer life span for adults. But the equilibrium between the factors affecting life and death results in population stability. The absence of harsh winters and migration eliminate two of the main causes of death for birds in temperate zones. On the other hand, the plundering of eggs and chicks is extremely high in the tropics. Various hypotheses have been advanced to explain this fact. It has been suggested that the serious threat of plunder may limit clutch sizes, which would explain why fewer eggs are laid (the fewer laid, the fewer lost). Moreover, a clutch with a large number of chicks would require constant comings and goings for feedings, and these repeated movements would greatly increase the risk of betraying the nesting site. This last hypothesis has been rejected because of lack of knowledge of the evolutionary mechanism which would have linked clutch size to risk of predators.

MIGRATORY MOVEMENTS

Migration refers to the regular, seasonal movement of bird populations from nesting sites to wintering areas. A third of the species in Thailand are migrants, characteristised by their habit of breeding in other regions (temperate, arctic, but also tropical) and, for the great majority, remaining in Thailand during the so-called winter period (this can last from July to May).

Migration originated because of the progressive extension of the area of distribution of birds. Conditions for survival throughout the year being unfavourable, birds were obliged to return regularly to their region of origin, at least during the difficult period. One theory concerning northern hemisphere species is based on the hypothesis that the birds may have sheltered in the more clement southern zones in order to escape the rigours of the Ice Age. Following the climatic changes, they may have tended to leave the southern regions to re-occupy their northern territory, assuming the constraints of migration after an absence of many tens of thousand of years. If glaciation were an important influence on the habits of the birds, it represents only one of the many influences in the development of migration.

'Long distance' migration between the northern and temperate regions of Eurasia and southern Asia is relatively well defined. As a general rule, birds breeding in western Europe make for Africa, those breeding in central Siberia spread through the Indian sub-continent as far as Sri Lanka, and those nesting east of longitude 90°E in east Siberia and China migrate to Southeast Asia, as far as the Philippines and Australia. There are exceptions to this broad pattern, for instance the Arctic Warbler, which nests in Siberia, Scandinavia and Alaska, only winters in tropical Asia.

The principal migration routes cross Southeast Asia, avoiding long sea crossings. One goes through China towards Taiwan, then to the Philippines and the Sundas. Another route, passes over the mainland, via China and Indochina, through Thailand and eventually along the Malaysian peninsula in the direction of Sumatra. There is another minor route from China to Vietnam that crosses the South China Sea to Malaysia.

The migratory birds seen in Thailand do not all come from the same latitudes. Although the majority are from the arctic, northern and temperate regions of Eurasia, others, such as the Purple Sunbird and the Silver Oriole, come from sub-tropical zones and from the north of tropical Asia. Breeding groups in the south of China, Laos and Burma are also able to migrate to Thailand and join up with the resident populations, such as the Ashy Drongo, the Black Drongo or the Black Bulbul. Others migrate between tropical and equatorial zones, sometimes even staying within the borders of one country. The Blue-winged Pitta nests in Thailand in the rainy season then travels to Malaysia and Indonesia to avoid the dry season. Similarly the Black Bittern and Hooded Pitta migrate to the peninsula in the dry season and return to breed on the mainland in the rainy season. There are other migratory paths, like that of the duck, which, after nesting in the central plain, migrates west in the direction of Bangladesh.

For some long distance migrants from the north, like the waders, Thailand is often only a stopping place between wintering and breeding sites. These autumn and spring stops allow the birds to build up their reserves of energy in order resume their migration over long distances.

Most long distance migrants live in the tropical zone between September and May, equivalent to approximately 70% of their life span. From this point of view, the breeding site appears to be almost a marginal habitat in their annual cycle. We might ask ourselves what advantages the birds find in crossing half the world to regain the inhospitable regions of the Arctic in spring when they could easily feed and accumulate sufficient fat reserves in their wintering sites. And yet, the mass of food available in the northern regions makes the trip worthwhile, providing the travelling birds with what they need to breed successfully.

In the tropics, as on their return to their breeding sites, the migrating birds must have the capacity to adapt rapidly to their new environment. Although there may be similarities between the vegetation in their breeding and wintering sites, like the mud flats, reed beds, bushes and forests, it is just as likely to be completely different, bearing no resemblance whatsoever to the region of origin. For instance, while the Arctic Warbler and the Eastern Crowned Warbler leave the northern conifer forests to winter in tropical forests and mangroves, the water warblers are often found in dense undergrowth.

Certain migrant species reproduce the social organisation from their breeding site in the tropics. Thus the Great Reed Warbler or the Brown Shrike appear to defend a territory in their wintering site. On the other hand, the waders and the buntings modify their social structure and adopt a gregarious type of behaviour outside the breeding season.

The population of Little Egrets in the coastal areas is composed of both migrants and residents.

The Birds and Their Environment

Species have evolved over a long period of history and the process of evolution continues to this day. Over the years, most species have adapted themselves to their surroundings, making the most of all the resources in the environment. A forest bird, therefore is not adapted to live in a rice field, just as a bird from the plain must adapt to living in the mountains.

Although oversimplified, the association of animal species with their environment constitutes a definite point of reference for the birdwatcher.

TOWNS AND VILLAGES

First contact with birds

The first birds one discovers are, naturally, those that live close to human habitation, in towns and villages, gardens and fields. These birds should not be overlooked, even if their abundance sometimes makes them commonplace.

Town birds are a good starting point because they open themselves to

The Kaeng Krachan National Park is a spectacular landscape of forests and hills.

frequent observation at close range. Once familiar to the birdwatcher they can serve as a point of reference for identifying other species.

Built-up areas are not a natural environment for birds, however, they do offer favourable conditions for some types of birds which are able to find some similarities with their natural habitat in buildings or gardens. The House Swift and the Pacific Swallow, for example, originally associated with rocky cliffs, today have colonised the facades of buildings. The Magpie Robin and the Scarlet-backed Flowerpecker find a vegetation which is familiar to them in the thinly planted woods and flowering trees in parks. Martins and starlings use lawns as a substitute for grassy clearings and fields.

In Bangkok, one still sees a few species in the gardens of residential areas and the parks surrounding government buildings and temples. Early in the morning, Lumpini Park is a great place to stroll and observe different birds, such as the Blanford Bulbul, the Pied Fantail, the Common Tailorbird, sunbirds and, during the winter months, various migrants from the north, such as warblers and flycatchers.

IN THE COUNTRY

The patchwork of habitats forming lands capes in the countryside is the result of years of human development. Despite this, in many casesa number of birds inhabiting the countryside have found similarities with their natural environment—stubble and fallow land for the birds of the savannah; waterways and flooded ricefields for the water birds; copses and orchards for the birds of the open forests. This re-created environment, however, shelters only a small number of the original bird population, and only the most ubiquitous have been able to establish themselves close to humans. Moreover, the variety of avifauna often only reflects the variety of landscape. Thus, the large areas of monoculture where rice, manioc, rubber or oil palms are grown, offer far fewer possibilities for observation than land consisting of small plots used for polyculture and raising livestock.

Even the beginner birdwatcher can pick up the shapes of the Black Drongo, the Indian Roller, the Green Bee-Eater or the Stonechat perched on a wire or

post along the roadside. Near fields and grazing cattle, one might also see a family of starlings or mynas, a pair of doves and, in the tall grasses, a coucal.

The flooded ricefields and the pools of water remaining after the monsoon regularly attract egrets, pond herons and wintering or passing waders. Rice ready to be harvested attracts grain eating birds, such as munias, weavers and mixed groups of buntings, which can also be found in the stubble.

Groups of passerines consisting of bulbuls, flycatchers, sunbirds, Common Iora, and Magpie Robin can be seen moving through bamboo hedges and copses.

The Black-shouldered Kite and the Shikra hunt in the sky. Large raptors, such as vultures, which used to glide over the countryside, have now largely disappeared.

ON THE EDGE OF THE WATER

Ponds, marshes and rivers

The development of agriculture and urbanisation have considerably reduced the number of marshy areas but a few large lakes and small ponds remain. Flooded ricefields provide another water environment which, even though seasonal, is still favoured by waterbirds.

In reed beds and other swampy vegetation live skulky species, such as rails, crakes and bitterns, which can only be seen with difficulty during their furtive forays into the open. Reed warblers give themselves away by their

The dry rice fields of Phrae in the north.

alarm calls and sometimes come to perch on the end of a tall stem. Supported by their long toes, jacanas, moorhens and Purple Swamphens can be seen walking on floating water lilies.

During the breeding season, the Lesser Treeduck and the Cotton Pigmy Goose live discretely in the swampy vegetation. In the dry season, groups of these duck in the company of other migrating species, such as Garganey and Common Pintail, assemble in areas of open water. In January, thousands of Garganey and Lesser Treeduck can be seen on Lake Borapet (Nakhon Sawan) or on the pond of Nong Waen game reserve near Chaiyaphum.

Formerly, the marshes sheltered large water birds, such as storks, ibis, pelicans and the Sarus Crane. These species seem to have been particularly vulnerable to the destruction of their habitat and have in large part disappeared. It is still possible to come across individual migrants or birds of passage which do not breed in Thailand—Asian Openbills, along with egrets, night herons, pond herons and cormorants take refuge in the courtyards of Buddhist temples.

The gravel pits and river sandbanks shelter a special avifauna, such as River Terns, Stone Curlews, Great Thick-Knees, River Lapwings, Pied Kingfishers and Small Pratincoles. These species have diminished greatly because of the disruption caused by human settlements. Nowadays, on a winter stroll along the river bank, away from protected areas, one can see species which adapt more easily to the environment, such as kingfishers and small waders.

The coast

Mention of the coast of Thailand immediately conjures up images of an exotic paradise with sandy beaches lined with coconut palms. For birds, these beaches are a relatively barren environment, missing the nutritional elements required to develop an abundant microfauna. However, do not be surprised to see species with particular feeding habits, such as sandplovers, which run briskly along the sandy expanse, quickly seizing their prey from the flat surface.

The muddy beaches, less attractive for the tourist, are an extremely fertile environment. The rich sediment of organic material which slowly accumulates in sheltered areas, such as bays and estuaries, form a particularly rich silt sub-strata. The proliferation of animal and vegetable matter attracts numerous passing and wintering waders, which regulate their activities by the ebb and flow of the tides. At high tide waders find refuge on small exposed islands, salt marshes, fish ponds and in mangrove trees. At low tide, they spread out over the exposed mud flats to feed.

Mangroves

Mangroves develop along muddy coasts and river estuaries. Mangrove trees are perfectly adapted to life in a salty or brackish environment. To counter the lack of oxygen in the mud, these trees have developed a system of aerial roots. The *Sonneratia,* which colonises recent deposits of sediment, has roots with extensions vertical to the air. The more spectacular *Rhizophora* has roots which protrude from the trunk and form a branching arc before going back into the soil.

Spawning and breeding grounds for numerous species of fish, crustaceans and molluscs, the mangroves represent an economic resource not yet sufficiently recognised, as the few remaining mangroves in Thailand testify.

Few species of birds are restricted exclusively to mangroves, except the Brown-winged Kingfisher and the Mangrove Pitta which never leave them. Collared Kingfishers, Mangrove Whistlers and Flyeaters can be seen outside the mangroves but never venture far. The rest of the species to be found are ubiquitous forest birds.

The rocky coast

The rocky coast and small islands are used as shelter for colonies of terns. Sea trips are an excelllent opportunity to study marine birds, such as the frigate birds or the rarer skuas.

Curiously, there are few sea birds in the warm waters of Southeast Asia. This relative paucity has not yet been explained satisfactorily, but one reason put forward is the elevated temperature of the surface water. Nutrients, and the whole trophic chain on which they depend (phyloplankton, zooplankton, fish etc), lie in the cooler water several metres below the surface, out of the reach of fish eating birds.

The Nicobar Pigeon and the Pied Imperial Pigeon are two species which are strictly insular and only live in the shelter of vegetation on islands off Thailand.

IN THE FORESTS

A group of Brown-headed Gulls at rest on the shore.

The abundance of fauna to that of the flora and the complexity of its structure. Consequently, it is in the forests, particularly the evergreen forests, that biological diversity is most pronounced and the greatest variety of birds is found. In Thailand, the majority of breeding species live in the forests. This single observation shows the importance of the conservation of the forests for the survival of birds.

Between the tropical continental area and the equatorial peninsula, there are various formations in the forest mantle juxtaposed on surfaces that have sometimes been reduced, depending on the soil, climate or the local particularities of the terrain. The patchwork of the forest has increased under the influence of humans, who have cleared it either partly or wholly.

Deciduous forests

Deciduous forests flourish when rainfall is low and the alternation between the dry and rainy seasons is well defined. The trees protect themselves against a deficiency of water by losing their leaves in the dry season. Two types of deciduous forests can be identified:

The dry dipterocarp forest is an open forest with relatively well spaced trees, allowing for the development of savannah undergrowth. Regularly plagued by bush fires, the

31

physiognomy of the forest changes through the seasons—from bare trees and burnt soil in the dry season to greener landscapes in the rainy season. The trees grow in poor and porous soil where the rainfall is less than 1,250 millimetres and where the dry season lasts six months. Dominant tree species with broad leaves of the family Dipterocarp constitute the main vegetation. The bird community is little diversified in comparison with other types of forests, but consists of characteristic species, notably woodpeckers and other arboreal birds. Lineated Barbets, Golden-fronted Leafbirds, Eurasian Jays, Blue Magpies and cuckoo-shrikes commonly haunt the foliage. The Rufescent Prinia, one of the rare species of small size, inhabits the grassy undergrowth.

The mixed deciduous forest is a blend of deciduous and evergreen trees. It develops when the rainfall is heavier (between 1,250 and 1,850 millimetres). This forest can be found on a wide variety of soils, and on the plain as well as in the hills. On valley floors and along water courses it sometimes supplants the dry forest. The undergrowth is mostly bamboo. Teak (*Tectora grandis*) is one species characteristic of this forest, but it has been exploited so intensively that it has become rare in its natural state. Reafforestation programmes have been undertaken during recent decades, but the ecological richness of the original primary forests has disappeared.

The Shikra, a sparrowhawk found in the open forests.

The mixed forest is an intermediary one, the structure of which is determined by the proportions of deciduous and evergreen trees. More complex and varied than the dry forest, it also shelters more birds but does not have a particular species to itself. The shaded cover of the undergrowth favours small birds, insectivores and mixed feeders like the babblers and certain bulbuls, as well as those species associated with bamboo, such as the Yellow-bellied Warbler, the White-browed Piculet and the Bamboo Woodpecker. In the rainy season, when the fruit ripens, mixed forests are visited by other birds (hornbills, pigeons, orioles and broadbills) which are usually confined to evergreen forests in the dry season.

The evergreen forests

As the name indicates, these forests remain green throughout the year. The leaves of the trees do not all fall at once but renew themselves all year, which gives the impression that they never lose their foliage. Evergreen forests evoke luxuriant vegetation in successive layers and an exuberant animal and vegetable life.

The tropical rain forest is the lushest and most complex of the evergreen forests. Limited to the peninsula and to a lesser extent to some particularly humid zones of the southeast, it is characterised by high but constant temperatures, regular distribution of rain throughout the year and humidity approaching saturation point.

The forest is structured in several layers. The ground, which hardly gets any light, is covered with a litter of dead leaves and is bare of grassy vegetation. The cleared undergrowth, interspersed with the trunks of large trees, is scattered with thin bushes and palms. From the thick canopy formed by the large trees (about 35 metres high) emerge the giants with their streamlined trunks sometimes reaching as high as 60 metres. Numerous epiphytes, ferns and creepers develop and bloom in the light at the top or in the penumbra of the undergrowth.

The humid tropical forest of Malaysia, which is similar to the one situated at the extreme south of the Thai peninsula, constitutes one of the richest natural environments in the world. It is home to a diversity of vegetable species, and botanists have recorded more than 200 species of trees on one single hectare of primary forest. The complexity of the structure of the vegetation favours remarkably diversified resources, which are well utilised by the birds—187 species have been counted in two square kilometres of primary and secondary forest in the Thai peninsula.

The species are distributed in a horizontal manner, often settling in one particular layer of the vegetation. Terrestrial birds (pheasant, partridge) scratch at the ground litter in search of food, while in the undergrowth one finds babblers and thrushes. Flycatchers, drongos and trogons occupy the first open perches, catching insects on the wing. The canopy hosts broadbills, leafbirds, ioras, bulbuls and groups of fruit eaters—pigeons, parrots, hornbills and barbets.

In the mainland area where the tropical climate is more pronounced, the rain forest gives way to a similar formation, poorer in species—the **dry evergreen forest**. It is also found as a gallery forest along the edge of water courses through the deciduous forests. Less diversified, the dry evergreen forest has, nevertheless, a structure and function similar to that of the rain forest. A few deciduous trees are also found among the emergents and bamboos often invade the damaged and degraded areas.

The bird community, although composed of the same types of families, differs from that of the peninsular forest in that it has Indochinese characteristics from the east and Indo-Burmese from the west.

A dry evergreenj forest in Kaeng Krachan National Park in the southwest of Thailand.

The mountainous evergreen forest grows in altitudes above 1,000 metres. Dominated by oak and chestnut, it is not as tall as the other evergreen forests and its structure varies depending on slope and orientation. The dry slopes are covered with a scattering of low trees. In the valleys, the forest is denser and taller, with moss and epiphytes invading the trees.

Typical mountain birds can be seen, which share some similarities to the birds of the Himalayas and the mountains of southern China—sibias, parrotbills, certain babblers, song babblers, and the Lesser Racket-tailed Drongo. During the winter they are joined by the forest migrants, thrushes, flycatchers and warblers.

On the dry plateaux and rocky crests in the north and northeast of the country, a sparse forest with open undergrowth has developed, populated with conifers—**the pine forest**. Pure pine forests are rare and generally host very few birds, making them an extremely poor locale for birdwatchers. Pines, however, are frequently associated with the mixed deciduous forests, on the hills and, higher up, blend with the mountainous evergreen forests. In these mixed stands, the bird community is even more diversified and composed mainly of ubiquitous species.

Although not completely restricted to pines, the Giant Nuthatch and the Great Tit are often found there. In the southern part of the country the Great Tit is associated with a completely different habitat—the mangrove.

THE BIRDS OF THAILAND

1. LITTLE CORMORANT
(*Phalacrocorax niger*)   (52 cm)

The Little Cormorant is found more or less everywhere, in marshy inland areas and on the coast. Of the three types of cormorant in Thailand, it is the most widely spread, although not the most common.

A skilful underwater fisher, it swims with its wings close to its body and is propulsed by its webbed feet. It seizes its prey and resurfaces to swallow it. Unlike other water birds, and paradoxically for a diver, it does not secrete fatty substances to waterproof its feathers. This obliges it to dive at short intervals and then return to a perch in order to dry its feathers. When perched it adopts a characteristic posture, wings and tail spread out in a priestly stance.

The Little Cormorant is distinguished by its small size, short, thick beak and long tail. In breeding plumage, the throat is dark and there are white feathers on the head and neck. After breeding, the head becomes brown and the top of the throat white. Immature birds are brown with traces of white on the throat and the upper breast.

It nests in colonies in trees, often close to egrets and herons. The nest is a messy construction of branches piled up in the fork of a tree. It breeds in the central plain and disperses after the breeding season.

Internuptial

2. LITTLE HERON *(Butorides striatus)* (46 cm)

The Little Heron is a regular visitor to mangroves and mud flats, where it nests. In winter it can be seen, alone, in the bend of a river or on the banks of a pond in a forest.

Even though active during the day, it is unobtrusive and prefers to remain in the shadow of the mangrove trees, only appearing in the open at the end of the day. Whilst resting, it adopts a characteristic posture, with its neck tucked back into its shoulders. In a hunting position, it crouches with its body nearly horizontal and remains squatting and immobile before suddenly unwinding to seize its prey—small water animals, fish, crustaceans, frogs and insects.

This small heron, somewhat stocky, seems at first sight to be uniformly grey. In fact, it has an attractive plumage, finely made up of grey and green which contrasts with the black crown and long plume. The young have streaked underparts with brown marks on the wing feathers. The Little Heron does not nest in colonies as do other herons, although several nests can sometimes be found close to each other. It builds a solid platform of branches at the top of a tree, in which it lays three to four eggs.

3. JAVAN POND-HERON (*Ardeola speciosa*) (46 cm)

On the mud flats and shallow waters of the rice fields, the Javan Pond-Heron melds into the environment so well that it is barely noticeable. When it flies, spreading its white wings, it looks like another bird. It hunts standing in the watery vegetation, often in unripened paddy fields. It keeps quite still to take its prey, walking slowly hunched over the water. It feeds on water animals—frogs, fish and small crustaceans—but it will also snatch small insects on the surface of the water. Usually silent, it emits a caw when landing or taking flight, or to distance its fellows (hunting areas appear to be reserved). The Javan Pond-Heron lives in the central region. In breeding plumage, the back is slate-grey, contrasting with the tawny head and neck. The breast is more cinnamon. Non-breeding plumage is dull brown with streaked head and front, similar to that of the immature birds. It then becomes impossible to distinguish it from the Chinese Pond-Heron (*Ardeola bacchus*), which can be found in large numbers all over the country between October and April. Before flying north to breed, certain Chinese Pond-Herons acquire their breeding colours—the head, neck and breast become dark chestnut and the back grey. They are easily identified.

Internuptial   Nuptial

The Javan Pond-Herons gather on large trees to spend the night. They nest in small colonies, often with egrets, night-herons or cormorants. The nest is a heaped mass of branches built on bamboo or a tree, sometimes near temples. The birds find peace and quiet under the benevolent protection of the monks, guarantors of the Buddhist precept of respect for animal life.

4. CATTLE EGRET
(Bubulcus ibis)   (51 cm)

Less aquatic than the other herons, the Cattle Egret particularly appreciates the presence of cattle, capturing insects and other small animals disturbed by the movement of the cattle in the grass. This close association helps the Cattle Egret greatly in its search for food. In winter, during migration it is possible to see Cattle Egrets throughout the countryside and the humid zones of Thailand, but the breeding grounds are restricted to the central region. The Cattle Egret breeds in mixed colonies with large waders, building a nest of branches in the trees. During this period, its head, back and breast become reddish brown. These colours appear progressively from mid-February. The non-breeding plumage is completely white and it is distinguished from other egrets by its stocky shape, squat neck and its thicker beak, the underpart of which has a prominent tuft of feathers.

5. GREAT EGRET
(Egretta alba) (90 cm)

Egrets, so striking with their white livery, move about in open spaces and are easy to see. Their immaculate plumage, visible from long distances and seemingly a disadvantage is in fact a particular adaptation for these aquatic predators.Five species have been identified in Thailand.

The Great Egret can be found on the coast as well as on lake shores and flooded paddy fields. It usually fishes alone in shallow waters,

6

watching, immobile, for its prey of mainly small fish but also amphibians, water insects, and crustaceans. It has a habit of looking at the water with its head sideways, avoiding the direct reflection of light from the surface. It is distinguished by its large size and long, angular, practically abnormal neck. In breeding plumage, it has a black beak, sometimes with a yellow base. The feet are black. It has long, soft plumes on its back, which fall to below the tail. In non-breeding plumage the plumes disappear and the beak becomes yellow.The Plumed Egret (*Egretta intermedia*), very similar, is smaller and its beak remains yellow throughout the year.

The Great Egret nests in very localised colonies in the central plain. From October to May the local populations are enlarged by winter visitors. Egrets, like other herons, are dependent on wetlands and their arrivals and departures are determined by the availability of water.

5 Internuptial

6. LITTLE EGRET *(Egretta garzetta)* (58 cm)

The Little Egret prefers shallow, open water. Along the coasts it keeps to the mud flats, salt marshes and fish farming ponds. Inland, it frequents swamps and flooded paddy fields, when the fields are first watered and the rice is planted. It fishes for small aquatic animals, punctuating each step with a swaying head and seizing its prey by the sudden stretching of its neck. The feeding method depends on its habitat and the availability of prey. Thus on the mud flats, with small fish stuck in the mud pools, it dashes about with its wings half open. Its beak and legs are black and its feet yellow. In breeding plumage, it has long filmy plumes on the breast and back. There are two long narrow plumes on the nape. The Little Egret nests in colonies, mainly in the central region, often in the company of other species. The nest is a light structure of branches in the trees. After breeding, the birds fly off south and to the peninsula. In winter, their numbers are augmented by migrants.

41

7. ASIAN OPENBILL
(*Anastomus oscitans*)   (81 cm)

Of the seven species of stork which originally nested in Thailand, the Asian Openbill is the only one to maintain a significant presence. The populations of the other species have diminished dramatically in recent decades, due to the combined effect of human persecution and lack of proper areas for refuge. This stork feeds on molluscs and almost exclusively on a fresh water snail (*pila*) which it finds in the paddy fields and marshes. The space between the two mandibles in the centre of the beak facilitates the seizing and holding of the shell. In flight, the storks extend their necks. For long-range flights, Asian Openbills use the warm ascending air currents and fly high in the sky. On arrival at their destination, they have a spectacular way of dropping down from the sky like a parachute, feet dangling. The Asian Openbill breeds in a few rare colonies in the central plain. Those of the Temple of Wat Pai Lom (Pathum Tani) and of San Lon (Saraburi) are the most important and benefit from protective measures. With the exception of some individuals which remain all year, this stork only stays in Thailand to breed.

The breeding season begins in November with long displays. The nests, at the top of trees or bamboos, are made of branches and the interior is regularly lined with green leaves. The concentration of nests can be very high, for example, 69 nests have been counted in a single tree. The female generally lays four eggs.

In April, the birds begin to disperse and start to migrate towards the west, to the deltas of the Ganges and the Brahmaputra.

8. LESSER TREEDUCK
(Dendrocygna javanica)   (43 cm)

The Lesser Treeduck is the most widespread of the four species of ducks breeding in Thailand. They can be seen on stretches of water of any size as long as there is an abundance of water plants. In flight, the head and neck are slightly inclined at a distinctive angle to the body. The dark underparts of the wings appear almost black and contrast with the lighter body. Its call is a slightly shrill whistle which accompanies its rapid wing beat. This duck is mainly vegetarian and eats floating vegetation and seeds. But it does not scorn occasional animal food (larvae or small vertebrates). It prefers to eat at night in paddy fields and marshes.

In the dry season, the Lesser Treeduck gathers on stretches of water, sometimes in large groups of several thousand birds amongst which can be seen many wintering ducks. In the rainy season, they disperse over the vast flooded areas and start breeding. The nest is made in a hollow tree or on the ground, hidden in vegetation. It is left bare or lined with down or dry leaves. The female lays about 10 eggs.

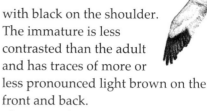

9. BLACK-SHOULDERED KITE
(Elanus caeruleus)   (33 cm)

An elegant raptor, typical of the cultivated plains and other open areas, the Black-shouldered Kite is easily recognised by its long, pointed wings and by its very light plumage with black on the shoulder. The immature is less contrasted than the adult and has traces of more or less pronounced light brown on the front and back.

The Black-shouldered Kite hunts large insects as well as small rodents and reptiles. It flies methodically over its hunting territory, hangs still with its feet down and tail spread before dropping with a flap of its wings on to its prey. Or, lying in wait on one of its usual perches, it searches the vegetation below. Present everywhere in Thailand, it is, however, most common in the central plain. The nest is built in a tree and forms a little eyrie of branches lined with more delicate vegetation. Three to four eggs are laid.

10. BRAHMINY KITE
(Haliastur indus)   (48 cm)

The Brahminy Kite was once a common sight along rivers and large swamps, often even in towns, but has now practically disappeared from inland regions. It can be seen mainly near the coasts, especially surrounding fishing ports, in mangroves and in river mouths. Fairly sociable, it flies around in groups, moving with slow wing beats. Largely a scavenger, its diet is eclectic. It readily eats the carcasses of small birds and dead fish, scraps from the fishing grounds and other detritus from the surface of the water. It also captures frogs, reptiles, young birds and large insects.

The adult is easily recognisable with its contrasting brown and white plumage. The  immature is dull brown with streaks, easily confused with the Black Kite (*Milvus migrans*), a raptor with similar behaviour. This latter can be distinguished by its more slender shape, dark plumage and strongly forked tail.

The nest is a structure of branches lined with assorted objects and is often built at the top of a tree in a mangrove, preferably near water. The female generally lays two eggs.

Immature

Adult

secondary vegetation and open country.

Sparrowhawks are distinguished by their small wing span, rounded wings and long tail which enable them to move rapidly among trees. Their hunting technique is based on surprise. Hidden in thick foliage, they swoop suddenly on their prey. The Shikra eats lizards and large insects. During the dry season, it takes advantage of the bush fires and hunts the insects which appear at the edges of the flames, often in the company of other species such as drongos, rollers, and bee-eaters. The male Shikra is blue-grey on its back and white finely streaked with rufous-brown on the front. It can be distinguished from other male sparrowhawks by its paler plumage and grey cheeks, contrasting with the darker crown. The white throat is divided by a narrow grey line. The larger female has a brown back with a greyish tinge. The immature is darker brown on the back with a lighter brown spotted underside. During breeding, circular flying displays over the territory are common. The bird alternates a series of slow glides with sudden dives and flutters, the shivering wings pointed downward, clearly showing the white bristling under tail feathers. These displays are often punctuated by sharp calls. The nest is a construction of branches lined with leafy twigs, protected in a tree. Three or four eggs are generally laid.

11. SHIKRA
(*Accipiter badius*)   (30-36 cm)

The Shikra is the most common of the three sparrowhawks resident in Thailand (four other species are winter visitors). It only breeds in the mainland of the country and migrates in small numbers to the peninsula in the winter. It inhabits open forests and can also be found in

12. CRESTED SERPENT-EAGLE *(Spilornis cheela)* (51-71 cm)

The Crested Serpent-Eagle is the most common of the eagles in Thailand and can be seen in all types of forests, on the plain and in the hills. Its noisy behaviour and distinctive pattern make it one of the most familiar raptors to any forest stroller.

When the temperature rises in the middle of the day, the Crested Serpent-Eagle wheels above the trees using the ascending warm air currents. It is then that one can hear, from time to time, its sharp call, a shrill prolonged whistling 'kwee-kwee', audible from afar. Although it can call at any time of the day from a perch, it has been noted that the stimulus triggering these calls is very closely linked to its soaring flight. In flight, it can be easily recognised by the large white band which emphasises the black edges of the wings and tail. On landing, the spotted white underparts and the thick crest which swells its nape can be seen. The immature has a paler head and front, the underpart of the wings finely streaked with brown and without the distinctive white band.

Perched on a high branch on the edge of a clearing, it lies in wait watching the movements of its prey on the ground. For the most part it captures snakes and lizards, but also large insects, small mammals and chicks. The Crested Serpent-Eagle breeds everywhere in Thailand, building its nest of branches in the cover of high foliage. The female only lays one egg.

13. CHANGEABLE HAWK-EAGLE
(Spizaetus cirrhatus) (56-75 cm)

The Changeable Hawk-Eagle lives in all types of forest, and from the plains to the mountains. It can usually be seen briefly flying across a valley or along a crest. Its shorter wing span (compared with the eagles of the open region), its large wings, its long and rounded tail indicate its adaptation to a woody environment. It perches, immobile, spying its prey—ground birds, mammals and reptiles—which it seizes on the ground. The plumage of the Changeable Hawk-Eagle differs from one individual to another, varying from a light phase, where the birds underparts are almost white, to a dark, uniformly brown phase. The long feathers on the nape, which do not form a real crest, give its head an angular profile. In the light phase, the whitish underparts with long black streaks differentiate it from the three other hawk-eagles of Thailand. In the dark phase it resembles the Black Eagle (*Ictinaetus malayensis*), but the latter has a black plumage, long angled wings and fine light streaks across the tail. Immature birds have completely white underparts and head.

In contrast to the Crested Serpent-Eagle, the Changeable Hawk-Eagle is rather silent, except during mating displays when it makes shrill, plaintive, prolonged calls. It engages at that time in spectacular flying displays during which it spirals up to a great height and then descends in a breathtaking dive.

The nest is a large platform of branches, regularly relined with green leaves, built high up in a tree facing an opening, overlooking a slope or a clearing. The female lays only one egg.

48

14. SIAMESE FIREBACK *(Lophura diardi)*   (female 60 cm, male 82 cm)

If one had to name the most dazzling species of bird in Asia it would undoubtedly be the pheasant group (peacocks, monals, junglefowl and pheasants). Eight pheasants, one junglefowl and one peacock live in Thailand, but each faces serious survival problems in varying degrees. Their status in Thailand is disturbing due to the serious disappearance of their habitat and to persecution by humans.

The Siamese Fireback lives on the plain in the undergrowth of some evergreen forests in the northeast and the southeast. Described as rather timid and once relatively common, it has today become rare in Thailand. Omnivorous, it pecks at seeds, fallen fruit, young shoots and buds, but also larvae, insects and worms which it obtains by scratching the litter. The male can be identified by its grey back, yellow, orange and red rump, and particularly by its completely black tail. The female is brown and does not have a prominent crest. The head and neck are brownish, the underparts chestnut-rufous streaked with white on the belly and flanks. The wings and back are broadly barred with black and tan. Of all the pheasants in Thailand, the female is the only one to have a strongly barred tail, which provides an excellent method of identification for a species which is often surprised in rapid flight through the undergrowth.

The Siamese Fireback lives and nests on the ground. During displays the male stamps around the female, claps and vibrates its wings, giving out deep clucks. The call is a repeated 'pi-yoo'. The female lays five to eight eggs.

49

15. RED JUNGLEFOWL *(Gallus gallus)* (female 43 cm, male 75 cm)

The Red Junglefowl, wild ancestor of the domestic cock, has played an important role in the history of humanity. The domestication of this bird, long ago, is today almost universal. Chickens were being raised in the Indus valley in 2,500 B.C. But it is likely that domestication took place much earlier in Southeast Asia and Thailand, dating from the first human settlements in prehistoric times. In Thailand, the Red Junglefowl lives in the forest, favouring bamboo woods from the plain to the mountains.
A terrestrial bird, it scratches the ground to find seeds, termites and other insects, worms and larvae. It is particularly fond of bamboo seeds and, in India, in a good flowering season the Red Junglefowl produces and raises bigger and earlier clutches.

The Red Junglefowl is extremely shy and only appears in the open in early

50

morning and late afternoon. If disturbed it hides under cover or flies off with noisy cackles to perch on a branch further away. Although not gregarious, it is not unusual to see a group of them. The cock's crow and hen's cackles are very similar to those of the domesticated birds. Audible at any time, the cock crows most frequently in the morning and evening. During the moult from June to September, it stays silent and its plumage becomes darker, losing the red hackles on the neck and the long tail feathers. The female is brown in appearance with golden streaks on the neck and black feet. The nest is a depression in the ground, lined with grass and dried leaves and protected by a cover of thick vegetation. The female lays three to six eggs.

16. WHITE-BROWED CRAKE
(Porzana cinerea) (20 cm)

The White-browed Crake was, until a few years ago, only known on the peninsula. However, recent observations have revealed its presence in the floating vegetation of open bodies of water in Bung Borapet (province of Nakhon Sawan) and in a part of the region near the Gulf of Thailand. Crakes are shy birds which stay under cover in marshy vegetation, only making brief sorties, usually in the early morning and at dusk. The White-browed Crake is, however, less shy and wanders about openly on floating islands of vegetation on the edges of reed beds until quite late in the morning. It feeds on shoots and seeds, water insects, larvae and small molluscs.

It is easily identified by its uniformly grey and pale brown plumage, and by the white streak across its head and eyebrow. The immature is more brownish and the white streaks on the head are less obvious.

Its call is a sharp and fluty whistle. The nest is usually near the ground or directly on it. It is made of reeds and grasses and lined with softer vegetation. Three to six eggs are laid.

51

17. PURPLE SWAMPHEN
(Porphyrio porphyrio) (43 cm)

This beautiful water bird, with its shimmering purplish-blue plumage, red beak and legs, prefers large stretches of calm water with thick floating vegetation bordered by reed beds. Its long slender toes keep it on these floating rafts which barely submerge under its weight. Occasionally the Purple Swamphen will climb small stems and bushes. It only swims a little and prefers to fly to cross a stretch of water.
Its calls consist of a nasal trumpeting, 'wak' and different raucous and muffled sounds. Often gathered in a small scattered group to feed, Purple Swamphens make small contact calls, 'chuk, chuk'. Food consists mainly of plants

complemented by molluscs and insects.
It nests in the rainy season and builds a large bowl of interwoven leaves and stems on floating vegetation or in the middle of the reed beds and bushes. The clutch varies between three and seven eggs.

18. WHITE-BREASTED WATERHEN
(Amaurornis phoenicurus) (32 cm)

The White-breasted Waterhen is common all around swamps, along ditches and small stretches of water, where the brushwood, bamboo thickets and the high grasses can give sufficient security.

It readily comes out of hiding in the morning and evening to search for food—water plants, small molluscs and insects—which it pecks at while walking. Its tail, held up while walking about, is agitated nervously from time to time, clearly showing the cinnamon under tail coverts. If disturbed it is reluctant to fly, but runs to cover. Immature birds are duller than the adults, with brown backs and greyish underparts.

The White-breasted Waterhen becomes particularly loquacious during breeding. It then makes a repeated raucous call 'kwak, kwak, kwak', preceded by groans, hisses and other curious sounds.

The nest, a shallow bowl of varied vegetation, is built on a tuft of grass or installed in a thick mass of bushes or bamboos. The female lays six eggs.

19. RED-WATTLED LAPWING
(Hoplopterus indicus) (33 cm)

The Red-wattled Lapwing lives in short and sparse vegetation near water, everywhere in Thailand apart from the northeast region. It paces around open spaces with jerky movements, stopping after each brief advance, pecking up insects with a sudden movement and straightening up directly. Its food consists of small terrestrial arthropods and worms. When disturbed, it flies a short distance giving a few calls and, once landed, continues its escape with long strides before stopping. Its fixed stance makes it difficult to spot, in spite of its bright contrasting plumage.

Its black head, marked with a white patch and a red wattle differentiates it from other lapwings.

During the breeding season Red-wattled Lapwings call to each other for hours, emitting their piercing call 'did-you-do-it', long into the night. It lays four perfectly mimetic eggs on the ground, in a natural depression. At the approach of an intruder, the adults can go into spectacular diversionary tactics. Simulating the inability to fly and giving plaintive calls they entice the predator after them in order to draw it away from the nest.

20. LITTLE RINGED PLOVER
(Charadrius dubius) (18 cm)

The Little Ringed Plover can be found inland as well as on the coast. It frequents the banks of rivers and streams, drying paddy fields and beaches of sand or mud.

In Thailand it is represented by two sub-species: *C. d. jerdoni*, resident, and *C. d. curonicus*, migrant. Their differentiation is based on biometrics (measurements of beak and wing) indistinguishable to the eye. The resident sub-species nests in pebbles by rivers in the north of the country. The eggs are laid amongst the pebbles with which they blend

19

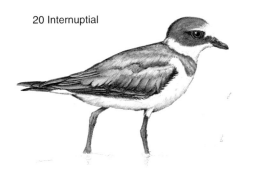

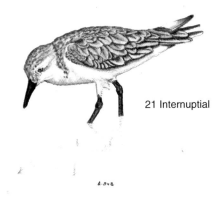

perfectly. This breeding population is reserved and sporadic. In fact, the Little Ringed Plover is mainly visible in winter when the northern migrants arrive. Its short beak prevents it from probing the mud and it pecks its prey (larvae, spiders, molluscs and worms) from the surface. It has a lively walking style, alternating short jerky runs with sudden stops. In non-breeding plumage it has a grey-brown back and white underparts with a beige pectoral band and a white collar. The forecrown is pale. In breeding plumage, the face is covered with a black band which goes over the white forecrown, and the breast becomes black. A bright yellow circle accentuates the contours of the eye. It is distinguished from other small plovers in flight by the absence of a white wing band. Immature birds look similar to non-breeding adults, but the pectoral band is reduced to two brown lateral spots.

21. RUFOUS-NECKED STINT (*Calidris ruficollis*) (15 cm)

The Rufous-necked Stint nests in the Siberian tundra. At the end of the breeding cycle it undertakes a long migration to South Asia and Australia. It can be found in groups on the coastal mud flats, feeding in the company of other waders. It pecks at the mud exposed by the tide, and scurries about looking for small invertebrates, larvae, worms and molluscs, giving up the search only when chased by the waves. When the tide comes in it finds refuge on exposed islands or on land. The Rufous-necked Stint is the most common of the stints. In non-breeding plumage the breast is an unmarked creamy-white and the upper parts a uniform grey. The feet are dark green, nearly black. In breeding plumage the head and neck are tinted rufous. Traces of this coloured plumage appear in springtime on those birds about to migrate. Two other similar stints can regularly be seen in Thailand— Temminck's Stint (*Calidris temminckii*) with a uniform grey-brown upper part, a grey chest, and yellowish legs that appear lighter; and the Long-toed Stint (*Calidris subminuta*) with light-coloured legs, a brown back with black marks and a chest lightly streaked with brown.

Internuptial

22. COMMON SANDPIPER *(Actitis hypoleucos)* (20 cm)

The Common Sandpiper is a rather solitary bird, keeping away from groups of other waders. It can be found on the edge of fresh or salt water, the banks of rivers and ponds and exposed estuarial and coastal mud flats.

It breeds in the north of China and eastern Russia, returning to Thailand during the winter. However, with delayed departures, early arrivals and summering of some individuals, they can be seen all the year round. The Common Sandpiper particularly likes the narrow bands of shore which border deep rivers, canals and ponds, and often perches on a stump in the middle of a river. The banks and beaches, between the pebbles, the roots and dead branches, are carefully explored in search of small invertebrates. It skims zigzagging across the surface of the water, alternating jerky wing beats with short glides. Its wings are pointed downwards showing a distinctive white band. It emits a fluting call of 'hididi' or 'tsi-wi-wi'. Landings are accompanied by head bobbing and a characteristic rise and fall of the tail. It has grey-brown upperparts. Fine brown streaks mark the sides of the head and the neck. White underparts extend as far as the back between the edge of the wing and base of the neck.

23. COMMON REDSHANK *(Tringa totanus)* (28 cm)

Breeding in Palaearctic regions, the Common Redshank migrates to Thailand in the winter. During its travels across land, it stops for a time in paddy fields, near bodies of water and rivers. However, like a number of waders it remains on the coast while in the tropics, and its feeding, dependant on the tides, continues through the day and night. At low tide, the Common Redshank spreads over the vast stretches of lukewarm mud in quest of food. Under the effect of the heat they appear no more than shimmering silhouettes with imprecise contours. The rising waters push them slowly back to the mangrove barrier, which they cross at high tide to regroup in the fish ponds and salt marshes with other waders. In the absence of other land refuges, they perch patiently on branches in the mangrove trees. During these rest periods they preen their feathers or doze with their beaks hidden in their back feathers. In flight, the Common Redshank can be identified by the large white band on the edge of its wing and its white rump. The tail is finely streaked. Immobile, its long orangey-red legs can be seen from a distance. Generally, the immature birds have lighter legs. When disturbed, the Common Redshank straightens up, legs stiffened, nervously nodding its head and neck. Just before taking flight, it emits its alarm call, a long and plaintive whistling 'tuht'. Its habitual call of 'tiu-du-tiu-du-du', often uttered in flight can be heard from afar.

Internuptial

57

24. COMMON GREENSHANK *(Tringa nebularia)* (35 cm)

During the spring and summer months, the Common Greenshank breeds in the wooded tundra and the pine forests of Russia. However, this large sandpiper from the north Palaearctic region also spends an important part of the year in the tropics. From the month of August it can be seen in Thailand near stretches of water and along the coasts, on the mud flats and on ponds of brackish water.

The Common Greenshank feeds in shallow water and on the soft mud at the water's edge, usually alone or in small dispersed groups. At times it catches small fish and crustaceans, at others it probes in the mud in search of molluscs and worms. The Common Greenshank appears very pale, grey-brown on top and white below. Its legs are greenish and its beak is dark, rather heavy and slightly turned up. During breeding, the top of the breast and flanks are streaked. In flight, the white triangle formed by the rump and back contrasts with the grey wing covering. The tail, which is finely barred, can appear white from a distance. Its call 'tiou-tiou-tiou', close to that of the Common Sandpiper, is harsh but not unpleasant.

At first sight the Common Greenshank can be confused with the Marsh Sandpiper *(Tringa stagnatilis)*, but the latter's shape is finer and more elegant. Its green legs are longer and its black beak is thin and straight.

Internuptial

25. BROWN-HEADED GULL
(Larus brunnicephalus) (46 cm)

Internuptial

Brown-headed Gulls arrive in Thailand in October. They come from lakes on the high plateaux of Central Asia where they breed. They winter along the coast, near estuaries and in ports, notably in Bangpoo where they regroup. They can also be seen on land near rivers and lakes.

Immature

They fly over murky water picking up all kinds of scrap left by human activities. Clumsy fishers, they make do with the occasional half dead fish.

In non-breeding plumage the

Adult

Nuptial

chocolate brown of the head is reduced to a dark patch on the ear with a few brown marks. The top of the wing is black with white spots. The immature resembles the adult in winter but the tail and wings are edged with black. The Common Black-headed Gull (*Larus ridibundus*) sometimes mixes with a group of Brown-headed Gulls. Smaller, it can be recognised by the triangular white wedge ending in a black line on the front of the wing.

26. GREAT CRESTED TERN *(Sterna bergii)* (46 cm)

Also known as sea swallows, terns are elegant birds, good long distance fliers and skilful fishers. More slender than gulls, they can be recognised by their forked tails, long pointed wings and short legs.

The Great Crested Tern flies over its fishing area scanning the waves, its head and beak pointing downwards, searching for fish. From time to time it suddenly dives, then resumes its flight, occasionally with its prey in its beak. Even though it has webbed feet, it rarely lands on water and seldom walks.

Gregarious by temperament, it readily lands on sand or rock with groups of other species, among which the Great Crested Tern is easily recognised by its size. It is a big tern with a solid look, a crown ruffled over its neck, a white forehead and a thick yellow beak. It can be confused, however, with the Lesser Crested Tern (*S. b. bengalensis*) which can be identified by its smaller size, thinner shape and orange beak. Purely maritime, the Great Crested Tern can be seen at sea and near coasts. It breeds in colonies on islands off Thailand and disperses at the end of the breeding season.

One egg, sometimes two, is laid in a depression between stones, forming a rudimentary nest lined with various materials.

Nuptial

27. WHITE-WINGED TERN (*Chlidonias leucopterus*) (23 cm)

A winter visitor, the White-winged Tern prefers to stay in the vicinity of the coast. In the company of the Whiskered Tern (*Chlidonias hybrida*), it enlivens the shallow salt pans and fish ponds with its capricious flying. But it does not scorn the fresh water swamps in the interior which resemble more closely its breeding environment. Unlike other terns, the

Nuptial

White-winged Tern snatches water insects and small fish from the surface of the water, without diving. It can be seen wandering alone over a swamp or paddy field, as well as in a group along an estuary.

In winter, its plumage is light grey above and white below, with just a few dark marks on the head. It has a distinctive white collar and rump. In summer, the head, body and under wing are pure black and contrast with the white on top of the wings and tail. The legs and beak are a bright red. When these terns arrive in Thailand or are preparing to return north, some moulting birds are streaked black and white. The two terns have similar non-breeding plumage. The Whiskered Tern can be distinguished by the absence of the white collar and rump. Its beak is thicker and tail more forked.

Internuptial

28. PINK-NECKED PIGEON *(Treron vernans)* (27 cm)

The Pink-necked Pigeon belongs to the Treron group, of which twelve kinds have been recorded in Thailand. They are fruit eaters with a predominantly green coloured plumage. The Pink-necked Pigeon is most common on the peninsula but has also been seen on the southeast coastal fringe and in the southwest region.

It frequents secondary vegetation, as well as mangroves and coastal plantations.

The Pink-necked Pigeon can be recognised by its light-grey tail with a dark terminal bar. The male has a grey head, a lilac neck and an orange spot on the lower part of its breast. The female is nearly all green with tawny under tail coverts.

The call is a modulation of hissing coos, which it makes in the foliage of trees. Gregarious outside the breeding season, the pigeons assemble in a group in the fruit trees with other fruit eaters (barbets, hornbills, mynas and fairy blue-birds) to share the harvest. They move with great agility to reach the fruit on the end of a branch. When alarmed they stop still or disappear into the greenery. When they take flight it is always surprising to see how many birds emerge from the same tree. The varied fruiting periods means that the birds have to move around locally. These movements, guided by the dependence on food supplies, can be on a large-scale in the dry season, taking the pigeons away from certain areas.

62

29. THICK-BILLED PIGEON *(Treron curvirostra)* (26 cm)

skin round the eye. They can be distinguished from other pigeons by the light-grey crown, brown back of the male and the beige under tail coverts, finely barred with olive-green, of the female.

The call is a melancholic coo of ascending and descending notes.

The Thick-billed Pigeon is the most common pigeon in Thailand. Present everywhere in the country, it frequents the forests of the plain up to the foothills, as well as the mangroves and secondary vegetation. Its arboreal and fruit eating habits are the same as those of other pigeons. It regularly flies down to the ground to drink or peck at the salty earth frequented by large mammals.

The two sexes can be distinguished from the rarer Pompadour Pigeon, *Treron pompadora)* by their thick beak with a red base, and the naked blue

A nest built next to an intolerant neighbour can lead to expulsion. Thus a couple of Thick-billed Pigeons which were building their nest near a Lineated Barbet were violently harried on several occasions and had to install themselves further away. To build the nest, the female perches in the fork of a branch hidden amongst the leaves. The male brings her twigs, one by one, from the surrounding trees. The female takes them in her beak and weaves a fragile looking platform around herself on which she lays two eggs, which the two adults take it in turns to hatch.

30. GREEN IMPERIAL PIGEON *(Ducula aenea)* (43 cm)

The Green Imperial Pigeon lives in the evergreen and mixed forests of the plain. Today its presence is sporadic, a consequence of the destruction of its habitat and hunting. It is occasionally seen, except in protected forests. Essentially a fruit eater, it flies around looking for suitably ripe fruit, often in small groups, after the breeding season. It has a fast, powerful and straight flight. On taking flight its wings clap noisily. The Green Imperial Pigeon can be picked out by its uniformly greeny-bronze upper parts and light-grey underparts, with rufous under tail coverts. Inthe hills of the continental area the Mountain Imperial Pigeon *(Ducula badia)* occurs. The Mountain Imperial Pigeon is bigger and has brown upper parts with a large light band on the end of its tail and light beige under tail coverts. As often with pigeons, the female Green Imperial Pigeon sits on a branch weaving the nest from the dried twigs brought to her by the male. During this period he sings more often. Hidden in the thick foliage he emits a deep cooing 'wouk-wouk-wou- hoor' which sounds from a distance like a rumbling.

64

31. SPOTTED DOVE *(Streptopelia chinensis)* (30 cm)

Often found close to houses, the Spotted Dove is common in the countryside up to the hills, in villages, suburban areas and coastal palm plantations. It feeds on seeds which it pecks at while searching scrub, bare land, or rice stubble. It also alights readily on dirt roads where, at the approach of a vehicle, it will fly off clapping its wings.

The pale shades of reddish-brown, grey and brown if the plumage, is set off by a large white spotted black collar. Its long tail is edged with white. The immature birds have no collar and are duller than the adults. The call is a sonorous cooing 'kou, kour, kour'.

The nest is a flat construction of small interwoven branches in a tree or a bush, occasionally in a building. The structure is so fine that sometimes the two white eggs or the chicks can be seen through it. In the north and northeastern regions the Oriental Turtle-Dove *(Streptopelia orientalis)* is also found. Larger and slightly redder, it has a patch of black feathers edged with light grey on each side of its neck. Further from humans than the Spotted Dove, it likes the open forest clearings and secondary vegetation of clearings abandoned by nomadic tribes.

Immature

Adult

32. RED TURTLE-DOVE
(Streptopelia tranquebarica) (23 cm)

The Red Turtle-Dove lives on the plains of the mainland region of the country. Smaller and stockier than the Spotted Dove, it frequents the same kind of areas and their habits are very similar. It is, however, shier and stays away from human habitation. Doves are popular as pets and can often be seen in cages at front doors, sometimes far from their place of origin.

The plumage is two-toned, the grey head and tail contrasting with the vinaceous-red body. A fine black ring marks the base of the neck. The outer tail feathers have a white border. Of the four turtle doves in Thailand, this is the only one that shows sexual dimorphism, the female being duller and browner than the male. The nest is a shallow cup of branches. The song is a deep cooing, repeated in a series.

The Red Turtle-Dove, like other birds, sometimes stands out in the sun in a characteristic posture with outstretched wings, tail open and puffed up feathers. One function of these sun baths could be to dislodge external parasites to accessible places for the bird to reach when preening, which usually follows these sessions.

♂

66

♀

33. GREEN-WINGED PIGEON *(Chalcophaps indica)* (25 cm)

This beautiful forest turtle-dove is often found on paths or near streams in humid and well shaded woods. The Green-winged Pigeon can be found everywhere in the evergreen or mixed forests as far as the lower mountain ranges. Somewhat solitary, it is unobtrusive and is often discovered by surprise. It gleans seeds, grains, fallen berries and dried fruits from the ground. It also goes to the salt licks trampled by large mammals in order to get the minerals contained in the soil. Flying low across the cluttered undergrowth at great speed, it only allows the observer a glimpse or flash of emerald green.

The sexes are different in colour. Although they both have metallic green mantles, vinaceous-red underparts and red beaks, the male is more brilliant and contrasted. He has a silver grey top on the head and white forehead and eyebrows. The immature is similar to the female. In flight, two pale grey bars mark the lower back.

Its call is a soft and melancholic 'kou-hooo' uttered at regular intervals. The nest is typical of pigeons, though more compact and solidly built. Placed in a young tree, in canes or a bamboo bush, it contains two eggs.

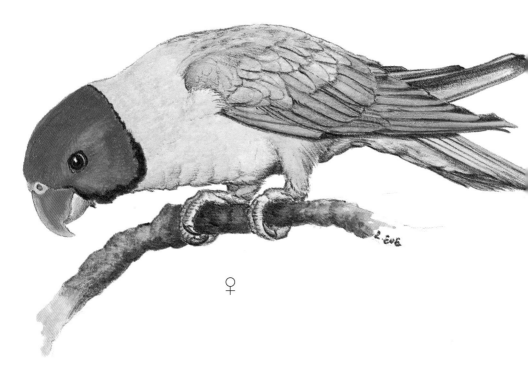

♀

34. GREY-HEADED PARAKEET *(Psittacula finschii)* (41 cm)

The Grey-headed Parakeet lives in deciduous and mixed forests and in woods of the plains up to the hills. It is confined to the northwest of the country, and to the cages of bird catchers.

It can be identified by its slate-grey head and green body. The male has a red patch on the shoulder. The immature is completely green with a black tipped yellow beak.

The parakeets move around in groups and fly fast and straight. Their particular shape—massive head and long pointed tail—and their strident calls make them easy to recognise. Mainly fruit eaters, they hang in noisy, nervous clusters on branches laden with ripe fruit and climb along the small branches hauling themselves up by their beaks at each change of step. They peck at more fruit than they can eat, allowing the rest to fall to the ground, supplying a providential meal for other animals.

The Grey-headed Parakeet nests in natural holes in tree trunks, or in old woodpecker or barbet holes. Sometimes it will hollow out its nest in worm eaten wood. Three to five eggs are laid.

The parakeets have, in part, been victims of their gregarious behaviour which makes them gather in large numbers in the cultivated fields and orchards (Deignan reported seeing, in 1936, a group of some 10,000 Red-breasted Parakeets *(Psittacula alexandri)* in paddy fields near Fang, in the north of the country). Slowly they were eliminated from the countryside and are now restricted to parks and nature reserves.

35. VERNAL HANGING PARROT (*Loriculus vernalis*) (14 cm)

This small green parrot blends so well with the foliage that it is easily concealed from view. Typically arboreal, the Vernal Hanging Parrot lives in evergreen and mixed deciduous forests, from the plain to the middle slopes of the mountains.

In pairs or small groups of five, six, or sometimes more, the parrots eat fruit and the nectar from flowers in the canopy. They move along the branches in acrobatic contortions often hanging by their feet, head down. They also adopt this strange position to sleep.
Both sexes are a bright green with a large red spot on the rump, orangey-red beak and yellowish legs. The male also has a blue spot on the breast. In flight, they can be recognised by their small compact shape, massive head and short tail. They also give themselves away by their constant rattling call 'tsee-sip' as they fly rapidly through the forest.

In the far south of the peninsula, the Vernal Hanging Parrot is replaced by the Blue-crowned Hanging Parrot,(*Loriculus galgulus*), differentiated by its black beak and greyish feet. The male also has a small blue crown, a red spot on the breast and a golden yellow mantle at the top.
The Vernal Hanging Parrot builds its nest in a hole in a tree which it lines with scraps of green leaves. The clutch is of three to four eggs.

♂

36. PLAINTIVE CUCKOO (*Cacomantis merulinus*)   (22 cm)

The Plaintive Cuckoo lives in open woodland and the secondary vegetation of the countryside. It can also be found in parks and town gardens, even in Bangkok, where its melancholic whistle can sometimes be heard through the cacophony of car horns and noisy motors. Less timid than the other cuckoos, it perches in the open, drawing out its long descending lament 'pwii, pwii, pwii, pi, pipilii'. It also emits other piercing whistles in a series of 'wii, tir, tlwii' in a rising crescendo. Its vocal activities can continue into the night. The adult has grey-brown upperparts with the head, throat and upper breast being grey. The rest of the chest and the belly are rufous-buff. The underpart of the tail is barred with white. The immature has a black barred body, rufous-buff above and paler below, certain individuals retaining this colour as adults.

37

♂

The Banded Bay Cuckoo (*Cacomantis sonneratii*), more of a forest bird, is difficult to differentiate from an immature Plaintive Cuckoo. The same size, they can be distinguished by their song and by the underparts of the body, the sides of the head and the whitish eyebrows with no rufous tint.

The Plaintive Cuckoo is an insect eater and feeds on caterpillars and other soft skinned insects.

It is a parasitic bird, laying its eggs in the nests of small insectivores, mainly warblers and tailorbirds. These foster parents then substitute themselves for the parent birds and hatch and feed the young until they can fly.

36

37. COMMON KOEL
(Eudynamys scolopacea)   (43 cm)

The Common Koel has a liking for thickets of wood and bamboo scattered around the countryside. It can also be found on the edge of mangroves or in trees.

It is mainly a fruit eater but will also eat insects. Discretely hidden in the high foliage, it normally escapes notice. Its presence is only signaled by its intrusive call of two syllables, 'ko-el', uttered at intervals or repeated in a rapid series reaching a crescendo.

Mating time provokes, apart from intense vocal activity, a lively agitation which dispels its normal reserve. The presence of a female near a male songster leads to some spectacular chases along large branches amongst the trees, and offers a wonderful opportunity to discover this large cuckoo.

The male is black with a blue gloss. The immature is like the female, brown spotted with beige and white on top and white streaked with brown below.

In Thailand, the Koel parasitises the Large Billed Crow (*Corvus macrorhynchos*) in particular. It mystifies its host by depositing its mimetic eggs in the clutch of those birds. If the chicks of the two species live in the same nest, those of the Koel will develop more quickly to the detriment of the others. This parasitism increases the crows's aggressivity towards the Koels, which are brusquely chased away.

♀

38. GREEN-BILLED MALKOHA
(Phaenicophaeus tristis)   (55 cm)

The Green-billed Malkoha lives throughout Thailand, in evergreen forests as far as the mountains, mixed forests and in secondary vegetation. It moves around in the shadow of the greenery, threading its way nimbly through the tangle of climbing plants and vines to find insects. It advances through the foliage, branch by branch, allowing an occasional glimpse of some part of its plumage before, in a short, gliding flight, it moves to another tree.

It can often be seen flying in bird waves and its frequent participation could lead one to suppose that it acts as a catalyst in this. Its solid build and long trailing tail disturbs insects, attracting other insectivores which are happy to follow it around. It has a red face, grey plumage, dark green wings and long graduated tail banded white. In the rain forests of the peninsula, it can be confused with the Black-bellied Malkoha *(Phaenicophaeus diardi)* (appreciably smaller with darker underparts). The Green-billed Malkoha emits a guttural, muffled and sobbing 'cok, cok'. Its rarely heard song is a clear whistle of six identical notes produced in less than a second. This non-parasitic cuckoo builds its nest deep in the shelter of a young tree or bush. The little cup of twigs, similar to that of pigeons, is lined with green leaves in which two to four eggs are laid.

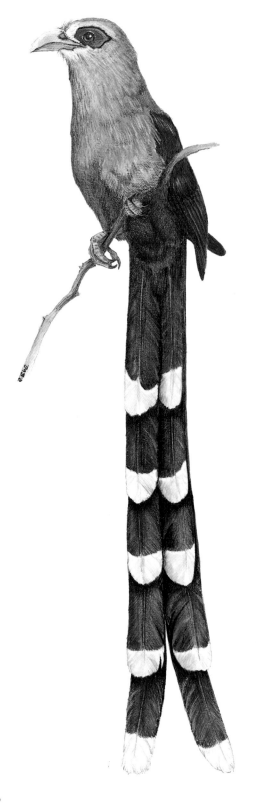

39. GREATER COUCAL *(Centropus sinensis)* (53 cm)

The Greater Coucal, a beautiful terrestrial bird with the look of a pheasant, belongs to the non-parasitic cuckoo family. It lives in grassy scrub and secondary vegetation, on the edge of forests and often near cultivated land and water. It flies low with slow wing beats and disappears in thick cover with a long glide. In the evening it sometimes perches out in the open on a bush above the vegetation.

While walking in the tall grasses and bushes it will eat any prey that presents itself (insects, reptiles, frogs, mammals, eggs and young birds). From time to time it will peck at some vegetation. Its call, one of the most familiar in Thailand, is a deep, resonant, low pitched 'poop, poop, poop, poop', uttered with the body pressing, and the head and neck twisted towards the ground. This stance helps spread the sound over a long distance, with the ground acting as an amplifier.

The contrast of brown and black is particularly distinctive in the adult. The immature is streaked with black on the brown parts and with beige on the black parts. Difficulties in identification arise from its similarity to the Lesser Coucal *(Centropus bengalensis)*, which frequents the same habitat. The latter is smaller (38 cm) and is distinguished by its song, a series of accelerating 'hoop, hoop, hoop' immediately followed by a cackled 't-t-tok-t-t-tok.

The underside of the wings is brown, not black as in the Greater Coucal. The solidly built nest of grass and leaves is attached to the stalks of seed plants or hidden in bushes. It can be spherical or semi-spherical in shape. To those carelessly assembled materials, leaves and stalks from nearby vegetation are knotted and woven into the structure without being cut. Thus, the nest always remains green and integrates perfectly with the vegetation. Three to six whitish eggs are laid.

73

40. COLLARED SCOPS-OWL
(Otus lempiji) (23 cm)

The strictly nocturnal habits of the Collared Scops-Owl make it difficult to see. It is, however, widespread in all woody areas, including those near human habitation, in parks and orchards. During the day it remains immobile and silent in the thickness of the vegetation.

A nocturnal hunter, it feeds mainly on large insects, occasionally capturing small rodents, lizards and young birds.

Its visual and auditory senses are well developed and adapted to darkness, and the large, closely set eyes capture the smallest ray of light. The disk of facial plumes focuses the most subtle noise towards its ears and augments its hearing capacity. The large wings are edged with a silky fringe which deadens the sound of air and allows muffled movements, inaudible in the relative silence of the night.

The plumage of the Collared Scops-Owl, the colour of bark and dead leaves, results in a remarkable concealment. The plumage varies from grey-brown to rufous, depending on the individual, and a pale half-collar marks the base of the neck. The two plumes on the forehead are prominent.

The Collared Scops-Owl utters a clear, monosyllabic 'pwaoo', repeated four or five times a minute and continued throughout the night until sunrise. It lays three or four eggs in a hollow tree.

41. ASIAN BARRED OWLET *(Glaucidium cuculoides)* (23 cm)

This little forest owl is not strictly nocturnal and is often active during the day. It lives in deciduous, mixed and open evergreen forests up to the mountains. It has also adapted to countryside with scattered trees. The Asian Barred Owlet is found everywhere except in the south of the peninsula.

Its brown body is finely barred with rufous-buff, the white belly streaked with brown and the throat marked with white.

It feeds on large insects and small vertebrates (rodents, reptiles and sometimes small birds) It can hunt at any time but generally keeps away from the active diurnal birds. The passerines sometimes react hostilely to its presence and harry it until it flies away. Bulbuls are often the original cause of this harassing, which attracts the curiosity of other birds, quickly creating a crowd.

It can be heard all day, but sings particularly at dawn. Its repertoire is a musical trill, evoking a celestial neighing as well as a soft barking on two repeated notes which rapidly get louder.

The Asian Barred Owlet nests in a hole in a tree, leaving it unlined, and lays four white eggs.

75

42. SPOTTED OWLET (*Athene brama*)

(20 cm)

The Spotted Owlet is a small, grey-brown owl, spotted with white on top and barred in front. It searches out natural cavities in old trees in the countryside and in parks and gardens near houses. It also likes stone and can be found in holes in walls and temple ruins. During the day it stays in the shelter of its hole, sometimes poking out its head, attentive to outside movement. It lives in the plain in the mainland part of the country, principally in the central region.

It hunts mainly for insects, rodents and small birds, worms and lizards. Like other nocturnal raptors, the non-absorbed food (insect shell, bones, skin, feathers) is compressed into a pellet which is regurgitated. Its vocalisations are varied, consisting of all sorts of calls, whistles and hisses. Three to five eggs are laid.

43. LARGE-TAILED NIGHTJAR
(Caprimulgus macrurus)
(30 cm)

The Large-tailed Nightjar is the most widespread of the six species of nightjar in Thailand. Present in forests, secondary vegetation and even in scrub, it can be found all over the country in the plain up to the mountains.At nightfall, its long-winged shape appears in the last rays of light, silent and rapid. With its winding and untidy flight, the Nightjar wanders in search of insects which it snatches on the wing. During the day, it stays in a tree or amongst the leaves on the ground, where its plumage and total immobility conceal it from view. Its short legs and small claws oblige it to crouch along the length of a branch. Confident of its mimetic stance, it only flies off at the last moment, and then very suddenly.

In flight, one can see a prominent white patch on the wing and on the edges of the tail of the male bird. These marks become buff on the female and are less visible. The smaller Indian Nightjar (*Caprimulgus asiaticus*) shares these same traits. Exclusive to the mainland, this bird prefers the drier, arid plains, mainly in the west of the country.

The Large-tailed Nightjar can be recognised particularly by its strange, resonant 'chonk, chonk, chonk', like a hammer on an anvil. It is uttered mainly at dawn or dusk from an open perch or from the ground. Certain mountain people call it the 'blacksmith bird' and believe that mastering the blacksmith's art is acquired by dreaming of this bird.

The Large-tailed Nightjar does not build a nest, laying its two eggs on the ground.

44. EDIBLE-NEST SWIFTLET
(Aerodramus fuciphagus) (12.5 cm)

The Edible-nest Swiftlet, a small swift with long, narrow wings, flies around the skies at remarkable speed with short and rapid wing beats. It feeds exclusively on insects, which it catches on the wing throughout the whole day.

It lives in colonies in caves and grottoes and moves around in the dark by echolocation. Giving brief 'clicks' which are reflected off the walls, these echoes allow them to judge distances and keep them oriented.

The Edible-nest Swiftlet nests in grottoes on the coast and on islands off the peninsula, sometimes in company with other close species of swift, the Black-nest Swiftlet (*Aerodramus maximus*). The morphological differences between the two (size and rump plumage) is too small to be of use as identification in the field. On the other hand, the colour of the nest, whitish for one and dark for the other, distinguishes them straight away. The nest is a little cup piled up against a rocky wall and built with the saliva produced by glands under the tongue, which swell up during the breeding period. On drying, this saliva hardens as an opaque, white cement in which the Edible-nest Swiftlet lays two eggs. This nest is a Chinese culinary delicacy. To satisfy demand, colonies of swiftlets in Thailand are plundered, their nests often being taken regardless of the stage of the breeding cycle. The Black-nest Swiftlet makes its nest by sticking its own feathers on with saliva. A single egg is laid. Previously, not much valued because of the impurities encrusted in the saliva, its nest has begun to be sought after for food.

45. ASIAN PALM-SWIFT *(Cypsiurus balasiensis)* (13 cm)

A uniform brown with a well forked tail, this little swift is typically associated with fan shaped palms, especially the sugar palms (*Borassus*) often planted on the edges of paddy fields.

The Asian Palm-Swift is found everywhere in Thailand and can be seen all year round near palm trees, chasing insects with its fast and agitated flight. It emits sharp and lively calls of 'bibiliti'.

The Asian Palm-Swift nests in small colonies under the dried palm leaves which remain hanging at the top of the trunks. The nest is usually stuck to the central vein of one of these hanging leaves. The small, shallow cup is made of vegetable down and feathers glued with saliva. Two eggs are laid.

46. ORANGE-BREASTED TROGON
(Harpactes oreskios) (30 cm)

The Orange-breasted Trogon lives in all parts of the evergreen and mixed forests, from the plain to the foothills of the mountains. It is unobtrusive, often alone and immobile in the shady undergrowth of the forest. It rests perched for extended periods on a branch with its head tucked between its shoulders. It has a habit of turning its back on observers and following them with an oblique look over its shoulder by imperceptibly moving its head round.

Mainly an insect eater, it snatches its prey on the wing by launching off its perch or prospecting in the foliage. Its short, thick beak allows it to cope with large, often tough insects. Of the six species of trogons in Thailand, the Orange-breasted Trogon is the only one without bright red in its plumage. Male and female have an orangey lower breast and yellow belly. The duller female has her grey head and upper parts tinted brown. Its call is a rapid succession of four or five soft and melancholic notes, 'teu, teu, teu, teu'. Once familiar, its song makes it easy to identify. The Orange-breasted Trogon lays two to four eggs in an open hole in a tree or at the bottom of a dead hollow trunk, usually low down.

47. COMMON KINGFISHER
(Alcedo atthis) (18 cm)

The Common Kingfisher is found near water, river banks, canals, ponds, on the edge of mangroves—anywhere with an open aspect. It is mainly a winter visitor, very common throughout Thailand during migration. Some breeding birds have been seen along tree lined river banks.

It is principally a fish eater, although it also catches amphibians, small crustaceans and water insects. Posting itself on an overhanging perch, it searches the water for the movement of small fish and dives, seizing its prey in a brief splash of water. Before swallowing its prey, it will bang it several times against wood or stone. The indigestible scales and bones are regurgitated as a pellet. It announces itself by a piercing and prolonged call, 'tiht...tiht...', often uttered in flight. The Blue-eared Kingfisher (*Alcedo meninting*), of similar size and plumage, is found in evergreen and mixed forests. This bird, however, is more intense blue and does not have a red spot on its ear.

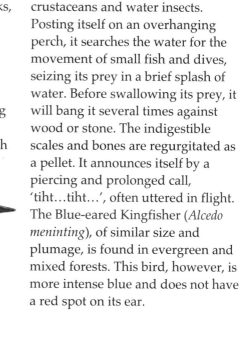

48. COLLARED KINGFISHER
(Halcyon chloris)

(24 cm)

The Collared Kingfisher is restricted
to coastal regions and river estuaries.
It has a particular liking for
mangroves where its call, a kind of
strident cackle of hoarse sounds,
often echoes in the trees. Its two-

toned plumage is remarkable, the upper blue-turquoise interrupted by a white collar and the underparts completely white. It mainly eats crustaceans, insects and amphibious fish which it captures in the swamps. The Collared Kingfisher generally nests in a hole in a tree or in a mass of earth and wood formed by ants' or termites' nests. More rarely, it nests in a tunnel in a river bank. When they hollow out the hole themselves for their nest, the male and female fly full tilt, beak first, into a rotten tree to make a small hole, which they enlarge by digging through the rotted wood with ther beaks. Four eggs are generally laid.

49. WHITE-THROATED KINGFISHER
(Halcyon smyrnensis)   (28 cm)

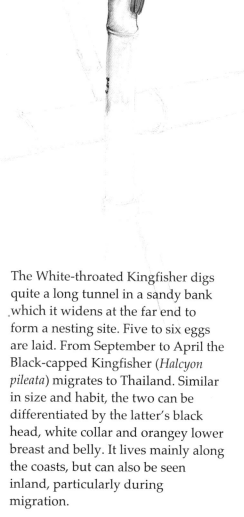

More impressive in size and particularly loquacious, the White-throated Kingfisher is familiar in the countryside and in open areas. Although not strictly associated with water, it is hardly ever far from it, and can be seen near paddy fields, marshes and river banks. It is easily identified by its large red beak, and brilliant blue, white and brown plumage. In flight, a large white spot can be seen on the wing.
Its call is a powerful, strident and rapid kind of laugh made interminably from a perch or when in motion.
It is an eclectic feeder with a preference for insects, but also reptiles, frogs and other small animals. It only occasionally eats fish.

The White-throated Kingfisher digs quite a long tunnel in a sandy bank which it widens at the far end to form a nesting site. Five to six eggs are laid. From September to April the Black-capped Kingfisher (*Halcyon pileata*) migrates to Thailand. Similar in size and habit, the two can be differentiated by the latter's black head, white collar and orangey lower breast and belly. It lives mainly along the coasts, but can also be seen inland, particularly during migration.

50. GREEN BEE-EATER *(Merops orientalis)*   (20 cm)

The Green Bee-eater is a bird of open country, near marshy areas and paddy fields. Apart from the peninsula, it can be seen everywhere in Thailand. Of a sociable nature, the birds stay in couples or small groups using electric wires, fencing or any other free, horizontal perch to rest on.

In flight it alternates fast wing beats with long glides. Its pointed wings, streamlined shape and elongated tail feathers enable it to catch the fastest insects (hymenopteras, dragonflies) with ease. The smaller insects with no shell are swallowed whole. Larger or more poisonous insects are taken back to the perch and killed before being swallowed with a small backward tilt of the head.

Calls are a rolling liquid 'tree-ee, tree-ee, tree-ee', usually made in flight.

It is differentiated from the other five bee-eaters found in Thailand by its predominantly green plumage with bronze highlights on the head and a fine black band at the top of the breast. The immature birds are duller, sometimes with a yellowish throat, and do not have elongated central tail feathers.

The Green Bee-eater nests in a long hole in crumbly or sandy soil. It excavates the earth with its beak and pushes it out backwards with its feet. Four to seven eggs are laid in the nesting site, often at the end of a tunnel, and the young remain there until they are ready to fly.

51. CHESTNUT-HEADED BEE-EATER
(Merops leschenaulti)

(23 cm)

The Chestnut-headed Bee-eater frequents light woodland and secondary vegetation from the plain up to the middle mountain slopes. Its behaviour, flight, calls, method of hunting and nesting are similar to those of the Green Bee-eater and, more generally, to those of the *Merops* group of bee-eaters. Unlike the Green Bee-eater, it does not have elongated central tail feathers. Its plumage is more vividly contrasted—the bright red of the head and upper back stands out against the pale blue rump and the yellow throat ends with a reddish band underlined with black. Immature birds are duller, without red on the upper part of the back. It breeds during the dry season and lays five or six eggs. In steep, sandy river banks, holes are excavated horizontally, whereas on flat land they are dug at a gentle slope. The nests are loosely arranged in a colony, spaced according to the type of ground and the spread of vegetation. It utters its call frequently while active, but becomes very discrete when returning to its nest. It makes its approach in stages, in the shelter of the trees and then, after a long inspection from its perch, descends directly to the nest.

85

52. INDIAN ROLLER (*Coracias benghalensis*) (33 cm)

Perched, the Indian Roller appears dark, of a uniform, almost dull colour. In flight, the brilliant blue wings and tail are suddenly visible. Common in open spaces, cultivated areas, scrub and on roadsides where some large trees survive, it can also be seen on the edge of clearings in open forests. Resident everywhere in Thailand it is, however, rarer in the peninsula. It is conspicuous on the bare branch of a tree, a mound of earth, a pole, an electric wire or any other point from where it can overlook an open space. It watches the movements of small creatures (insects, reptiles, small rodents, etc.) which it captures on the ground by dropping on them. More rarely, it catches insects on the wing. The formation of couples and territorial demonstrations begin in January and lead to spectacular aerial acrobatis. Giving harsh, croaking calls, the Rollers roll, glide, spin and dive in the sky. Sometimes, when nothing is disturbing the peace of the territory, they will suddenly take off in a direct line, making numerous calls, before returning calmly to their perch, having chased off an imaginary intruder. The nest is built high up in the hollow of a tree trunk and lined with a variety of matter. The clutch is usually three eggs.

The Dollarbird (*Eurystomus orientalis*) is more of a forest bird than the Indian Roller. It frequents the edges and clearings of forests where it perches silently in big trees. It can be identified by its dark, nearly black plumage contrasting with a large red beak. In flight, a circular white patch is visible on its wings and it is this resemblance to the American banknote that has given it the name of 'Dollarbird'.

53. GREAT HORNBILL
(Buceros bicornis) (122 cm)

The size of the Great Hornbill and its huge curved bill, surmounted by a protruding casque, evoke the gigantism and peculiarity of prehistoric creatures. The powerful and heavy wing beat produces a noisy blast in the air. Its impressive call, a sort of barking roar, resounds and spreads far through the forest. Its ecological needs oblige it to live in thick evergreen and mixed forests, which, today in Thailand, are limited to a few protected areas. This explains its precarious

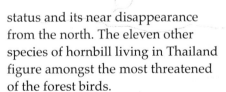

status and its near disappearance from the north. The eleven other species of hornbill living in Thailand figure amongst the most threatened of the forest birds.

The Great Hornbill mainly eats fruit (figs), but also eats animal protein, particularly during the breeding season, (insects, gastropods, reptiles, mammals and birds).

The nesting habits of hornbills are unique—the female walls herself into a hole in a tree to lay and hatch her eggs. With or without assistance from the male, she slowly closes up the hole using a cement made of regurgitated food, droppings, wood shavings, sawdust and earth. She only leaves a small opening through which the male will pass her food. She lays one or two eggs and remains captive for the whole incubation period, moulting during this time. She leaves the nest before the young can fly and helps the male in feeding them.

Out of the breeding season, the hornbills sometimes form large groups. One such group of 70 Great Hornbills, was recorded in the National Park of Khao Yai.

54. INDIAN PIED HORNBILL *(Anthracoceros albirostris)* (73 cm)

More widespread than the other hornbills, the Indian Pied Hornbill adapts to a variety of woody environments, even those partly degraded.

Two sub-species of Indian Pied Hornbill occur in Thailand. *A. a. albirostris*, which is present in most of the country, has outer black tail feathers edged with white. *A. a. convexus*, recorded in the extreme south of the peninsula, has completely white outer tail feathers. Often in small groups, flying from tree to tre one after another, Indian Pied Hornbills signal their presence by their sharp and persistent cackling. They also fly down to the ground to have collective dust baths to rid themselves of external parasites.

They eat mainly fruit and readily join up with other frugivores (other hornbills, pigeons, barbets) in trees with ripening fruit. They also include insects, reptiles and other small mammals to their diet.

Mating starts in January with the choice of nesting site by the couple.With successive comings and goings between the hole of choice, the male invites her to follow him, and presses his invitation by sometimes regurgitating food into the hole.By way of accepting, the female approaches and inspects the future nest site. Offerings of food and mating take place close by. As with other hornbills, the female walls herself in during incubation and until the young can fly.

55. BLUE-THROATED BARBET (*Megalaima asiatica*)   (23 cm)

The Blue-throated Barbet is a typical bird of the canopy. Constantly hidden, it signals its presence over a long distance by incessant and monotonous calls, 'tookarook, tookarook, tookarook'.

Its calls are omnipresent. It is restricted to the evergreen forests of the lower hills of the north and southwest and in some areas of the peninsula. Principally a fruit eater, it also eats large insects found in the foliage. To nest, it makes a hole in a dead tree trunk or uses a woodpecker's old nesting site.

The Blue-throated Barbet can be distinguished from the 12 other species of barbets by its blue face and throat, and its red forehead and crown divided by a dark blue band. The majority of barbets have a bright green body and the multicoloured pattern of the head is the only means of identification. This is why the recognition of calls, different for each bird, often constitutes the only method of identification of any use in the field.

The Blue-throated Barbet is very similar to the Blue-eared Barbet (*Megalaima australis*). The latter, smaller (17 cm), has blue on top of its head and its throat, a black forehead and three red patches on the sides of the head. Its call, 'ko-tek, ko-tek' can be repeated 120 times a minute. It can also give a monosyllabic whistle, which is unusual for a barbet. It lives in the foliage of evergreen and mixed forests and of secondary vegetation, in the plain up to the mountains.

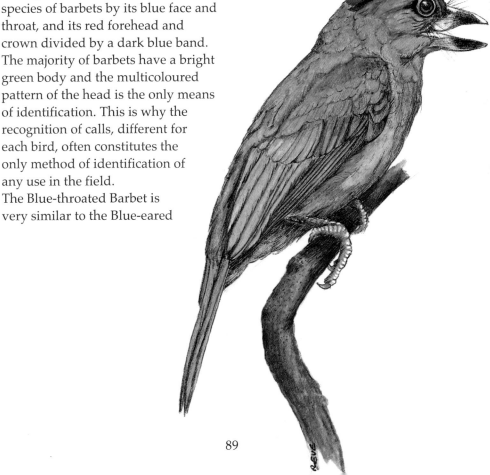

56. LINEATED BARBET (*Megalaima lineata*) (28 cm)

The Lineated Barbet is a familiar silhouette in the deciduous forests. It also lives in secondary vegetation and in open woodlands. The usual coloured head of the barbet is replaced in the Lineated Barbet by streaked plumage as far as its belly. The beak and orbital area are yellow. Lineated Barbets are known as fruit eaters, however, their diet consists largely of insects, especially in the breeding season. They search underneath the leaves at the end of branches and capture, not without difficulty, stick insects, cicadas and praying mantis. They also take advantage of the hatching of flying termites, which they snatch in the air above the forest.

Extremely loquacious, especially during the breeding season (February to May), they have a repertoire of several sounds of which two are repeated continuously—the first, audible mainly in the morning and evenings, is one repeated note, while the second is more elaborate and often stimulates a response from other birds. This call starts with a long, throaty trill, prolonged by a series of repeated notes, the first singer being immediately followed by others, provoking a chain reaction. These choirs are particularly intense at the end of the day. Another call, 'too-ta', is sometimes made during the day. The couple digs a hole in a tree trunk or uses an old woodpecker nesting site, such as that of the Greater Yellownape (*Picus flavincuha*). The female lays two to four eggs. The young are fed by both adults which often arrive at the nest together. As one distributes the food, the other waits patiently close by, to feed the young once the way is clear. The young fly after about five weeks and their plumage is hardly distinguishable from that of adults.

90

57. COPPERSMITH BARBET
(Megalaima haemacephala) (16 cm)

The smallest of the barbets in Thailand, the Coppersmith Barbet is a common resident of deciduous forests and open woodland, of the countryside where there are copses and of urban parks and gardens. It is even found in mangroves.

The feeding and breeding habits of the Coppersmith Barbet are similar to those of other barbets. Often perched on top of dead wood, from where it can see more clearly, it has also been seen perched on the small hand of the clock of the Bangkok central post office at nine o'clock. The Coppersmith Barbet is green above and streaked below. The black and yellow face is heightened by a red forehead, and the yellow throat and upper breast are separated by a red band. The plumage of the young birds, little different from the adults, is distinguished by its duller colours. The call is composed of one single note 'tonk,' unflaggingly repeated in a regular rhythm, though it sometimes gets carried away with excitement. From time to time it sings, one note to the left and another to the right, thereby adding to the dispersion of its resonant message.

58. LACED WOODPECKER *(Picus vittatus)* (30 cm)

The Laced Woodpecker is found in a variety of forests and secondary vegetation to the north of the Isthmus of Kra.

Like all other woodpeckers it has a remarkable morphological adaptability which enables it to exploit the resources of tree trunks and branches. Supported by rigid tail feathers, claws gripping the bark, it makes a detailed inspection of the interstices of the wood. Climbing jerkily up the trunk, it eats insects and larvae living in the wood, then descends to search the stumps and raid ant and termite hills. At rest, it perches on a horizontal branch, in the same way as other birds.

It moves among the trees with an undulating flight, alternating brief series of wing beats with oblique dives, accompanied by usual calls of a sharp 'kyip', or a sonorous giggle on a descending scale. It makes a hole in a tree to lay its eggs.

The Laced Woodpecker has throat and breast of the same colour, with the rest of its underparts streaked. These characteristics differentiate it from the Streak-breasted Woodpecker *(Picus viridanus)*, restricted to the peninsula and the forests along the Burmese border, and the Streak-throated Woodpecker *(Picus xanthopygaeus)*, which lives in deciduous forests in the southwest of the country, both of which are completely streaked on the front.

59. COMMON GOLDENBACK *(Dinopium javanense)*   (30 cm)

The Common Goldenback can be found anywhere in Thailand, in a variety of habitats such as deciduous and mixed forests, mangroves and secondary vegetation.Often in couples, the Common Goldenbacks search the tree trunks for insects and frequently participate in bird waves with other woodpeckers, drongos, laughingthrushes and smaller birds, such as bulbuls. They eat vegetable matter, fruit and seeds. To dislodge insects buried in the wood, woodpeckers are sometimes obliged to use inefficient stratagems. Trying to get at a beetle hidden in a long tunnel with two entrances, a Common Goldenback drums on one side to persuade the insect out of the other entrance and then flies round to catch it. After several attempts, the faster insect often escapes. The Common Goldenback nests in a hollowed-out hole in a tree trunk in which two or three eggs are laid. Mating is a noisy game of chase through the trees, accompanied by frenzied movements of the head and wings, the red feathers ruffled. It is surprising how similar the plumage of the Common Goldenback and the larger Greater Goldenback *(Chrysocolaptes lucidus)* is when these two birds are relatively distant genetically. The Common Goldenback has only three claws whereas the Greater Goldenback has four, implying an ancient

differentiation. In the wild, they can be distinguished principally by two black malar stripes on the Greater Goldenback. The female has a black crown with white spots which is white streaked for the female Common Goldenback. The two birds are often found in the same habitat and their calls are an important element in identifying them. Although in flight they produce similar piercing notes, the call of the Common Goldenback is a harsh, fast trill, whereas the Greater Goldenback's sounds more like the strident noise of the cicada.

93

60. GREY-CAPPED WOODPECKER
(Picoides canicapillus) (15 cm)

Notable for its small size, the Grey-capped Woodpecker is able to explore dead wood and the most inaccesible branches. It is found more or less everywhere in Thailand as far as the mountains, open forests, mangroves and secondary vegetation.

They often mix with flocks of insectivorous birds, such as nuthatches, flycatchers, small cuckoo-shrikes, leafbirds and bulbuls. Always moving, they drum the wood actively, flitting from one branch to another, with a preference for the narrower ones. They eat insects and larvae principally, but will not turn down fruit pulp and nectar from certain flowers.

The Grey-capped Woodpecker can be identified by its grey crown, black back barred with white and streaked underparts. The male has a small red patch above its eye, hardly visible in the open. It often announces its presence with a sharp trill 'chilui, chilui' and also by drumming on dead wood.

Like other woodpeckers, it nests in a hollowed-out hole in a tree and lays three to four eggs.

61. BLACK-AND-RED BROADBILL
(Cymbirhynchus macrorhynchus) (25 cm)

Of the seven sorts of broadbills in Thailand, the Black-and-Red Broadbill is the most threatened. It can still be found near rivers, evergreen forests and in the secondary vegetation of the plain of the southwest, southeast and the peninsula. The destruction of its habitat has already brought about its disappearance in several areas of the southeast. Perched on a high branch in the undergrowth, immobile and unobtrusive, it only betrays its presence by its long, guttural, ascending trill. Its large coloured beak contrasts with the deceptively dark appearance of its plumage. Short flights from point to point display the white mark decorating the wings. It eats mainly insects which it captures in the foliage or on the wing, but also benefits from the proximity of rivers to eat small aquatic animals. The nest, typical of broadbills, is suspended from a branch over a stretch of water or a gully. An untidy mess, the construction is in fact very elaborate. It is made of leaves, grasses, roots and moss in the shape of a pear, and fixed to the branch by a long tie. The side entrance is sheltered by a small canopy and a long stalk extends the bottom of the nest.

62. BLUE-WINGED PITTA *(Pitta moluccensis)* (20 cm)

Brilliantly coloured terrestrial birds, pittas have a secretive character which makes them interesting to naturalists. Twelve species occur in Thailand. They often prefer to remain hidden during the day, and the first glimmer of daylight is the best opportunity to see them on the paths of the forest. When disturbed, the Blue-winged Pitta runs hopping, sometimes leaping, out of sight. Otherwise it will fly a short distance, showing the conspicuous white mark on its wing, and take refuge on a low branch or small headland before disappearing.

It searches for food in the ground litter, scratching the earth and disturbing the dead leaves to find the worms and arthropods hiding beneath. Recognising the call is an important way of discovering the presence of pittas. That of the Blue-winged Pitta is a double whistled note, the second higher in tone. Blue-winged Pittas arrive in Thailand in April or May with the first rains to breed in the open forests. The nest is a spherical construction of bamboo leaves (or other plants) and twigs and has a side entrance. Often by a stream, it can be built near a tuft of bamboo or in the hollow of a dead tree. The nest generally has four or five eggs. During the dry season most of the Blue-winged Pittas migrate to the equatorial regions of Malaysia and Indonesia. During migration they can be seen in a more varied environment (secondary vegetation, mangroves, plantations). In the mangroves of the west coast of the peninsula, the Blue-winged Pitta is associated with the Mangrove Pitta *(Pitta megarhyncha)*, a strictly resident bird. The latter, very similar, can be distinguished, however, by a thicker beak and the near absence of the black line on top of the head.

63 Nuptial

64

63. BARN SWALLOW *(Hirundo rustica)*   (15 cm)

The Barn Swallow is principally a winter visitor to Thailand, though a few rare breeding colonies have been seen recently in the mountains in the extreme north of the country. It can, however, be seen all year round as the migratory movements extend over a long period and appear to overlap. The numbers are lowest in June, when most of the birds are breeding in China, Siberia and Korea. Visible everywhere, the Barn Swallows prefer the inhabited areas of the plain, where they criss cross the skies snatching insects on the wing. At nightfall they come together in large groups in reed beds of swamps or on electric wires and aerials in towns. In Patpong, Bangkok's most lively nocturnal area, some 280,000 Barn Swallows gather each night between November and April. During its stay in the tropics, the Barn Swallow moults completely and only continues on its northerly migration once it has its new feathers. The immature birds, which constitute a large part of the population, have a duller and less contrasted plumage. These and the adults, deprived of the long feathers in their tails, have a very similar silhouette in flight to that of the Pacific Swallow *(Hirundo tahitica)*. Moreover, the sub-species *H. r. tyleri* has pale red under parts not white, as with other breeds.

64. PACIFIC SWALLOW *(Hirundo tahitica)*   (14 cm)

Restricted to the coastal areas, and to islands off the peninsula and the southeast, the Pacific Swallow is a settled maritime bird. It perches on narrow, bare branches, wires and aerials, sometimes with the Barn Swallow. The brick red of the forehead is more widespread than on the Barn Swallow, and the throat does not have a black band underlining it. Underparts are greyish and it does not have long feathers on its tail. Its call is a light warble. Alarmed, it emits a piercing and repeated 'twiit'. It nests, alone or in colonies, in the shelter of rocks or of varied buildings. The nest is a shallow bowl constructed with mud and filled with dry grasses, lichen and feathers. The study over several years of a small colony of Pacific Swallows in Malaysia showed a surprising regularity in the breeding season, the date of the first egg laid being practically the same each year. This is particularly remarkable in tropical latitudes when the climatic (temperature, humidity) and cosmic (photoperiod) factors on which the rhythms of biological activity are based are constant all year round.

65. LARGE WOOD-SHRIKE *(Tephrodornis virgatus)* (23 cm)

The Large Wood-Shrike flourishes in all types of forests from the plain up to the middle slopes of the mountains. Sociable by nature and often in small groups, they are active among the branches, chasing insects and their larvae, especially caterpillars. They also join mixed feeding flocks of insectivorous birds, making incessant contact calls, a musical 'plui' amongst others. The song is a rapid repetition of 'pui, pui', which accelerates and rises in tone in the middle. The plumage of the Large Wood-Shrike, fairly neutral in appearance, is recognised by a black mask and a white rump. The female is more brown than grey on top and the facial mask is less contrasted. The immature birds have a brown upperpart scaled with black and beige. The nest is a shallow bowl of twigs, lined with softer vegetation, grasses and rootlets, built in the fork of a tree. Two to four eggs are laid. In the deciduous and mixed forests of the north, the northeast, and southwestern regions, the Large Wood-Shrike is sometimes found with the Common Wood Shrike *(Tephrodornis pondiceriamus)*. The latter, a smaller bird, has white eyebrows above the black band and white outer tail feathers.

66. SCARLET MINIVET *(Pericrocotus flammeus)*   (22 cm)

The Scarlet Minivet is found in all types of forests as far as the middle slopes of the mountains and can be seen in the open at the top of trees or at the end of high branches.

In families or small groups, they flit close to the tops of the trees, chasing insects which they catch on the wing. They also eat berries and nectar from flowers. They move from tree to tree, signalling their progress with sharp, perky whistles of two or three repeated notes 'twit, twit'.

The Scarlet Minivet is the largest of the eight minivets found in Thailand and can be recognised by the two distinct red patches on the wing, when at rest. The female is slaty-grey above and yellow below. The forehead, the two patches on the wing and the outer tail feathers are all yellow, while the wing is a slightly green tinted yellow. The immature resembles the female and, during the moult, the young males are coloured yellow and orange.

During displays, the male and female glide with spread wings, descending in a spiral before landing on the top of a tree. The nest is built high in a tree. Well camouflaged, it merges with the bark. It is a small shallow cup of lichen and other vegetation collected on the branches and strengthened with spiders' webs.

♀

♂

67. COMMON IORA *(Aegithina tiphia)* (15 cm)

The Common Iora lives in deciduous and mixed forests, mangroves, secondary vegetation, parks and gardens. It stays in the foliage, searching for caterpillars and insects along the branches. The Common Iora often announces its presence with melancholic whistles. Its repertoire consists of varied calls and songs, the most distinctive of which is a long quavering whistle (or several notes) finishing with a sudden inflexion, 'whiiiiii-tiou' or 'tui, tui, tiou'. During the breeding season the male plumage is dark above, sometimes completely black, and bright yellow below. The long flank feathers can rise to cover the rump which then appears white. For the rest of the year the male resembles the female, the black being replaced by green, and there are two white wing bars. The Common Iora's nest is a cup of finely interwoven grasses and fibres, strengthened on the exterior with spiders' webs. It is situated at various heights, in the fork of a tree or a bush. The size of the clutch is two, or sometimes three eggs. Two other types of Iora can be found in Thailand. The Green Iora *(Aegethina viridissma)* replaces the Common Iora in the rain forest of the peninsula. The Great Iora *(Aegethina lafresnayei)* lives in evergreen and mixed forests and can be distinguished by its larger size and lack of wing bars.

68. GOLDEN-FRONTED LEAFBIRD *(Chloropsis aurifrons)* (19 cm)

The Golden-fronted Leafbird is an arboreal bird which prefers deciduous and mixed forests and secondary vegetation on the plain as far as the foothills. It is not found in the peninsula.

The orange forehead differentiates it from the other four leafbirds in Thailand. It stays in the foliage where it is camouflaged by its leaf-green plumage. Active in its search for food, it looks particularly for flowering trees. It flushes out insects or gathers nectar from flowers as far as the end of branches, which it often grips upside down, in acrobatic postures with head hanging down. It also readily eats berries and, passing from one flower to another, helps pollination.

The Golden-fronted Leafbird has an astonishing ability to imitate the calls and songs of other birds. It can give successively the calls of drongos, bulbuls, ioras and even the Crested Serpent-Eagle, while inserting notes from its own repertoire. Its own song is a whistled melodious phrase, 'vi-tu, tieu, tieu, tieu, tieu, vi-tchit'.

During mating displays the perched male bends its legs and flaps its wings over its back with its tail spread out. The main structure of the nest is composed of dried grasses which the adults collect from the ground. While one collects the materials, the other keeps watch on a bush. The nest is built in a fork just below the top of a tree and is lined with mosses and soft vegetation. Three eggs are usually laid.

69. BLACK-HEADED BULBUL *(Pycnonotus atriceps)* (18 cm)

The Black-headed Bulbul likes evergreen, mixed forests and secondary forests, often preferring to be near water where the vegetation is more luxuriant. It can be seen in the plain and up to the middle slopes of the mountains.

The black head contrasts with the yellow underparts and the brilliant olive-yellow mantle. The tail is yellow-tipped with a black subterminal band. A few very rare individuals have slaty-grey breasts, bellies and tops of the back.

The Black-headed Bulbul moves around as much in the canopy as in the bushes. Its varied diet consists of fruit, berries and insects, which are caught on the wing. Musical twitterings generally accompany periods of activity. It also has a double whistled note, 'stii-ou'.

The nest is a fairly large bowl made of twigs, dead leaves and grass, placed fairly low in bamboos or in the fork of a shrub. Two to three eggs are generally laid.

70. BLACK-CRESTED BULBUL
(Pycnonotus melanicterus)   (19 cm)

During the hottest part of the day, when other birds are silent, the Black-crested Bulbul is still active and its crystalline notes can be heard in the calm of the forest, 'wheet tri, trippy wheett, trippy wheet'. Its calls stop suddenly in the middle of the afternoon and it stays very quiet until the evening.

It frequents the evergreen and mixed forests up to the higher mountains. The black head, raised crest and olive-yellow body differentiate it from all the other bulbuls. In the east and southeastern region, the sub-species *P. m. johnsoni* has a red throat. It eats berries, fruit and insects. But, as with those birds which have a mixed diet, the quantity of insects consumed rises during the breeding period.

In company with other forest bulbuls, they fly around with insectivores or visit fruiting trees. The Black-crested Bulbul builds a small nest of leaves and dried grass, held together on the outside by spiders' webs and lined with softer material. The female lays two to four eggs.

71. RED-WHISKERED BULBUL (*Pycnonotus jocosus*) (20 cm)

The Red-whiskered Bulbul is a bird of the open country and secondary vegetation, living in copses near cultivated areas, scrub and gardens. Sociable and noisy, its presence enlivens the parks of certain towns in the north, notably Chiang Mai where it abounds. Although widespread from the plains to the mountains, it is absent from the northeastern region and from the central plain near Bangkok. It is easily distinguishable by its black crest, red under tail coverts, white cheeks with a black malar stripe and red streak below the eye. Very loquacious, it emits short, musical whistles, 'wi-ti waet' as well as other, more grating calls. Its varied diet is composed of berries, fruit and insects. Outside the breeding season, the Red-whiskered

Bulbuls are gregarious. In the dry season, they disperse to establish their nesting territories. During mating displays, the male perches in a prominent position near the female, with its back rounded, tail fanned out and its wings gently fluttering. The nest is a bowl of twigs and leaves carefully tied up with spiders' webs and lined with soft grass, rootlets and horse hair. It is placed fairly low in a bush, in climbing plants and sometimes on odd supports near houses. Generally three eggs are laid.

72. SOOTY-HEADED BULBUL *(Pycnonotus aurigaster)* (20 cm)

The Sooty-headed Bulbul lives only in the mainland part of the country, in open forest, dry scrub and the orchards of the plain as far as the mountains.

It can be recognised most easily by its lightly crested black head and dusky white rump. Five sub-species have been identified in Thailand, among which *P. a. Thais*, present mainly in the southeast of the country, has yellow under tail coverts. The others, spread out over the rest of the country, have red under tail coverts. They feed on berries, fruit, nectar from flowers and insects, and occasionally search for ants and termites on the ground.

The song consists of short, melodious phrases, 'tirlup' or 'trep, trep, pre-tirlur'. The nest is typical of those of bulbuls, delicately woven and at a low height in a copse. The female normally lays two to three eggs.

In the middle of the afternoon in the dry season, the bulbuls, like many other passerines, fly down to refresh themselves in a spring or a pool. After drinking, they wade into the water up to their bellies and spray themselves generously with head movements and wing beats. They then return to a nearby perch and shake themselves well before smoothing their feathers.

73. YELLOW-VENTED BULBUL *(Pycnonotus goiavier)* (20 cm)

The Yellow-vented Bulbul is found mainly on the coast, irregularly venturing inland. It frequents coastal scrub land, palm groves, plantations and gardens. The white face contrasts with the black lore and brown top of the head. The yellow under tail feathers are the only bright bit of plumage.

The Yellow-vented Bulbul is both an insect and fruit eater and sometimes feeds on the ground. As garrulous as the other bulbuls, it strings together snatches of whistled phrases, such as 'tidloo, plu, pludluit' and harsher calls, making up a sort of medley. The nest is a cup of interwoven twigs and leaves lined with soft material built fairly low in the vegetation.

74. STREAK-EARED BULBUL *(Pycnonotus blanfordi)* (20 cm)

The Streak-eared Bulbul lives in open woods, scrub, near cultivation and in gardens. It is quite common in Bangkok, where it can be seen in parks and in the greenery surrounding houses. It can also be seen everywhere on the plain and as far as the lower mountain slopes. Its plumage is brown, paler below, with fawn under tail feathers. There are fine streaks on the side of the head. In the peninsula it can be confused with the Olive-winged Bulbul *(Pycnonotus plumosus)* which is darker, and has less visible streaks to the head and olive tinged wings. The Streak-eared Bulbul announces itself with rumbling guttural whistles, interspersed with more grating notes. It also has a musical trill.

Its diet is typical of that of bulbuls, frugivore and insectivore. Two eggs are laid in a nest made of twigs and leaves strengthened with spiders' webs and built in a bush, tree or climbing vegetation.

75. BLACK DRONGO (*Dicrurus macrocercus*)   (28 cm)

Travelling by road or train, one cannot avoid passing a Black Drongo perched conspicuously on an electric wire or on the back of a buffalo. Its black plumage and deeply forked tail make it particularly distinctive. One can also see a characteristic white spot on the corner of the beak. Common in all types of countryside and more generally in open spaces, it is only resident on the mainland of Thailand. During the winter, the numbers increase with the arrival of visitors from northern regions, which migrate as far as the peninsula. Outside the breeding season Black Drongos assemble in the evening in woods and bamboos, which they leave at dawn in an undulating flight towards their feeding grounds. Mainly an insect eater, the Black Drongo darts off its perch to catch insects on the wing. It sometimes catches them on the ground and will occasionally eat other small prey (reptiles and young birds). It returns to its perch in order to dismember its prey, holding it in place with its feet, before swallowing it up.

Its vocal expressions are powerful and varied, composed of numerous scraping, hoarse or metallic calls, amongst which can also be heard clear, melodious whistles.

The Black Drongo builds its nest high up in a tree. The cup, a loose structure of twigs, grass and leaves, is strengthened by spiders' webs. It is generally suspended in a fork at the end of a branch. The clutch varies between two to five eggs.

76. ASHY DRONGO *(Dicrurus leucophaeus)* (29 cm)

The Ashy Drongo frequents deciduous, dry and evergreen forests, mangroves and secondary forests from the plain to the middle slopes of the mountains. Both resident and migrant, it can be identified by its forked tail and its grey plumage which, depending on the six Thai sub-species, varies from light grey to nearly black. The sub-species *D. l. leucogenis*, a winter visitor, can easily be identified by its light grey plumage with white on the sides of the head.

The Ashy Drongo belongs in the canopy and will often perch on a bare branch above the foliage or on the edge of a clearing. Sometimes it descends to the ground or to grass level to feed. It takes off with ease to chase insects, showing a surprising agility in its flight.

The Ashy Drongo constructs a nest of stalks, lichens and grass in a fork below the tree tops in which three or four eggs are laid. During the whole breeding period and until the young can fly, one of the adults perches near the nest on watch and chases for a short distance all birds passing close by. The predators (raptors, hornbills, crows) are chased with a great deal of determination and recklessness. This aggressive behaviour towards predators, common to all drongos, probably encourages other species of birds to nest in the same area to benefit from their protection.

Occasionally it collects nectar from certain flowers as well as fledglings from their nests. Attracted by bush fires, it flies up high to catch those insects driven upwards in the columns of hot air above the flames.

Its repertoire is wide, quickly alternating sharp and discordant sounds, hoarse alarms and more harmonious whistles. It also incorporates fragments of calls and songs of other birds.

77. GREATER RACKET-TAILED DRONGO (63 cm, tail 30 cm)
(Dicrurus paradiseus)

Its distinctive shape, demonstrative behaviour and exuberant calls make the Greater Racket-tailed Drongo one of the most astonishing birds to be found in the forest undergrowth. It can be seen everywhere in Thailand, in all types of forests, usually of lower elevations. It has a preference for high, cleared undergrowth of vines and horizontal branches on which it can perch. It catches insects by its nimble and rapid flight but it will not scorn small animal prey and nectar from flowers. Like other forest drongos, it often joins bird waves. It can easily be identified by its plumage, completely black with a blue sheen, a tuft of feathers curved back to its forehead and elongated tail feathers ending in flat rackets. However, these two distinctive feathers are often worn out or missing. Even before the first light of dawn, the Greater Racket-tailed Drongo makes its combination of varied calls and metallic whistles. An excellent mimic, it is capable of imitating the calls and songs of other birds and incorporating them into its own repertoire.

The nest is a cradle of interwoven stalks, suspended between two branches of a fork. It generally contains three eggs which can be seen through the openwork structure.

Placed in a cleared space in the undergrowth, it allows the sitting bird to have a clear view all round. In that environment, it is visible from a distance and so must slip away at the least alarm. It remains close by, hidden in the vegetation, and will not hesitate to attack if interest is shown in its nest. In the evergreen forests above 800 m, the similar Lesser Racket-tailed Drongo (Dicrurus remifer) can be found. This smaller bird has a rectangular tail and does not have the prominent tuft of feathers over its beak. In spite of a slight overlap of their altitudinal range, the two birds tend to avoid each other.

109

78. BLACK-NAPED ORIOLE
(Oriolus chinensis)

(27 cm)

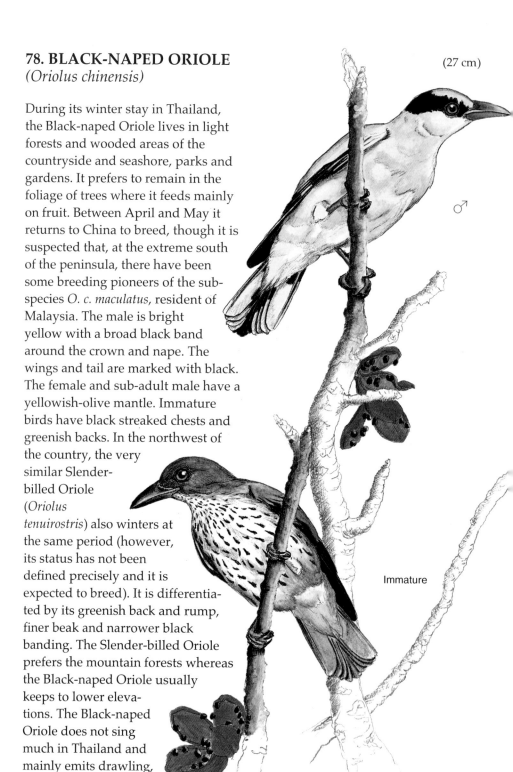

During its winter stay in Thailand, the Black-naped Oriole lives in light forests and wooded areas of the countryside and seashore, parks and gardens. It prefers to remain in the foliage of trees where it feeds mainly on fruit. Between April and May it returns to China to breed, though it is suspected that, at the extreme south of the peninsula, there have been some breeding pioneers of the sub-species *O. c. maculatus*, resident of Malaysia. The male is bright yellow with a broad black band around the crown and nape. The wings and tail are marked with black. The female and sub-adult male have a yellowish-olive mantle. Immature birds have black streaked chests and greenish backs. In the northwest of the country, the very similar Slender-billed Oriole (*Oriolus tenuirostris*) also winters at the same period (however, its status has not been defined precisely and it is expected to breed). It is differentiated by its greenish back and rump, finer beak and narrower black banding. The Slender-billed Oriole prefers the mountain forests whereas the Black-naped Oriole usually keeps to lower elevations. The Black-naped Oriole does not sing much in Thailand and mainly emits drawling, nasal calls of 'dyenn'. Its song is a fluty whistle 'doo-dlee-oo'.

♂

Immature

110

79. BLACK-HOODED ORIOLE *(Oriolus xanthornus)* (25 cm)

The Black-hooded Oriole is a resident of deciduous and mixed forests, and of secondary forests in the plain. In the peninsula, it is confined to mangroves. It prefers the foliage of trees, feeding on insects, fruit, berries and nectar of flowers.

The massive hatching of termites brings it flying out of the leaves to catch those insects which abound above the forest.

The adult has a black head, yellow body and wings and tail marked with black. Immature birds can be distinguished by their pale throat and chest streaked with black, and dark head with a trace of yellow on the forehead and round the eye. The most usual calls are a clear whistle of 'witit, oodloo-huhu', and 'houpoo-pli-diloo'. Other variations exist, like the resonant and penetrating 'ti-too'. More rarely, it utters a hoarse mewing sound. During the breeding season, the oriole is a tireless singer and its vocalisations predominate in the forest. The nest is a basket of vegetation hung in a fork and the female generally lays three eggs. After hatching, if the sun's rays bother the chicks, the adults will shade them by standing on the edge of the nest with their backs to the sun. Likewise, when it rains, they will sleep on the nest to protect the chicks.

80. ASIAN FAIRY-BLUEBIRD (*Irena puella*) (25 cm)

Strictly arboreal, the Asian Fairy-Bluebird lives hidden in the dense cover of the foliage of diverse evergreen and mixed forests, from the plain up to the mountains. It has a particular liking for the canopy of large trees over rivers.

It feeds on fruit for preference but will also eat nectar from certain flowers and, occasionally, some insects. It will often join other frugivores in trees with ripening figs. The male's brilliant blue upper parts make a dazzling contrast with the black below, often eclipsed in the poor light of the undergrowth. The female and the immature birds are a uniform verditer-blue. The Asian Fairy-Bluebird expresses itself mainly with brief, liquid, resonant calls, 'wee-woot' or 'tiu, wit-weet'.

The nest is composed of a platform of small branches heightened by a crown of rootlets and small stalks mixed with mosses. It is built by the female alone and is placed in a fork in the shelter of thick foliage. After the two eggs are hatched, the couple share in feeding the young birds.

112

81. BLUE MAGPIE *(Cissa erythrorhyncha)* (66 cm)

Once very common in deciduous forests and light woods, the Blue Magpie is relatively rare and localised today. It can be seen everywhere from the plain up to the middle mountain slopes, except in the central region and in the peninsula. The long blue and black shape and graduated tail make it highly distinctive. It usually flies around the large clear branches of the undergrowth but does not hesitate to take refuge at the top when disturbed. It also goes down to the ground where it moves by hopping, with its tail erect. It feeds on animal prey (insects, small reptiles, frogs and small birds) but will also eat seeds and fruit. Often in small groups, the magpies move around noisily, maintaining a continuous ringing contact of brief calls. They go from tree to tree, one after the other, alternating fast wing beats with short glides, their long tails waving in the wind. Their repertoire is extensive, composed of numerous variations of calls, hissings and clear whistles. The Blue Magpie often has a whistled 'tuuuuu, tut-tut'. The first, longer note, is followed by two or three short motifs. The nest is a structure of small branches, lined with softer material, placed on a horizontal branch or bent bamboo, often near an opening or a cleared space (a slope, the edge of a clearing). There are three to six eggs in a clutch.

82. LARGE-BILLED CROW *(Corvus macrorhynchos)* (50 cm)

The Large-billed Crow is a familiar bird in the towns, countryside and on the seashore, where it benefits from human presence. This commensalism does not, however, make it abundant, except locally. In the past, the House Crow (*Corvus splendens*), smaller and with a grey neck, was present in the province of Petchaburi. Today it has disappeared.

The Large-billed Crow is omnivorous, eating all sorts of animal and vegetable food and detritus. It is also a predator which on occasion attacks sizeable prey. When not an object of persecution, the crows can be very brazen. For example, in the zoological park in Bangkok, where they live in large numbers, they are often a big success with picnickers, who happily give them the remains of their food. Their powerful croaks, 'kraa, kraa', are characteristic of this bird family. The nest is a large structure of branches in a fork at the top of a tree, sometimes in a bush. Three to five eggs are laid, to which are sometimes added those of the Koel, a parasitic cuckoo.

83. VELVET-FRONTED NUTHATCH
(Sitta frontalis)

(12 cm)

The Velvet-fronted Nuthatch shows a remarkable turn of speed up and down trees, particularly head down. It can move easily in this fashion, because of the strength of its legs and, in contrast to woodpeckers and treecreepers, it does not need the support of its tail feathers. It moves around with little hops searching and hammering the bark with its beak to seize insects and their larvae. It lives in all kinds of forests up to the mountains. It often flies around with insectivores, announcing itself with a repetition of soft calls, 'tsitt, tsitt', often preceded by a trill. The Velvet-fronted Nuthatch is differentiated from the four other nuthatches in Thailand by its coral-red beak and a black patch on the forehead. Underparts are pale, white on the throat and pink on the belly. The thin black eyebrow found on the male is missing on the female. It nests in a hole in a tree and often has to alter the entrance. If the entrance is too narrow, it enlarges it with blows with its beak, if it is too large, it reduces it by cementing the entrance with mud. Inside, it places moss and down and lays three to five eggs.

♀

84. PUFF-THROATED BABBLER
(Pellorneum ruficeps)   (17 cm)

The Puff-throated Babbler lives close to the gound in forest undergrowth, bamboo and bushes, from the plain up to the mountains. Always hidden in vegetation, it is so unobtrusive it is often overlooked. It moves around by hopping and rumages amongst the dead leaves in search of insects, well planted on its relatively long and strong legs, adapted to its terrestrial way of life.

It has a powerful trisyllabic whistle which sounds like 'pretty dear'. The song is a long melancholic melody of descending and ascending whistled notes. This bird is heard in the morning and remains relatively silent for the rest of the day.

The adult has a dark rufous crown and a white eyebrow. The throat is white, often puffed out, and the underparts have dark brown streaks. The immature birds, rather duller, have no streaked underparts.

Placed on the ground near a clump or a bush, the nest is a bowl of fine grass hidden in a pile of messy leaves in the shape of a ball. Three eggs are laid. If disturbed near its nest, the babbler does not fly away but runs off like a small rodent. The mimicry is so perfect that one could mistake the identity of the animal.

85. WHITE-BROWED SCIMITAR-BABBLER
(Pomatorhinus schisticeps) (23 cm)

The White-browed Scimitar-Babbler can be found in all types of forest (deciduous, mixed, evergreen), bamboos, scrubland, in the plain and the mountains. Often in a small group, or in the company of laughingthrushes, it remains near dense cover and feeds on insects, seeds and berries which it collects while exploring the ground litter and tangled vegetation of the undergrowth. Occasionally it will search the foliage in the trees.

More often than not, the call is a series of 'hoot' repeated three to six times with varied rhythms.

Its yellow beak differentiates it from the four other scimitar-babblers in Thailand. Upperparts and belly are brown and the throat and breast white. The black band on the eye is topped by a white eyebrow.

The White-browed Scimitar-Babbler builds a dome of long bamboo leaves interwoven with grasses. This nest, lined with softer vegetation, is placed on the ground or slightly raised in a bush. The clutch is three eggs.

86. STRIPED TIT-BABBLER *(Macronous gularis)* (13 cm)

The Striped Tit-Babbler is particularly partial to the luxuriant vegetation which proliferates on the edges of forests, clearings, along roads and rivers. It can be seen everywhere in Thailand, on the edges of different evergreen and mixed forests as far as the mountains. In small groups, it is unceasingly active in the search for insects in the shade of the tangles of twigs and foliage formed by climbing plants and creepers. It makes frequent contact calls and often joins bird waves. Its characteristic call, a rhythmic succession of 'chonk, chonk, chonk,' invariably accompanies a walker along a road. In the shady foliage, the Striped Tit-Babbler often appears darker than it really is. The throat and breast are a pale yellow streaked with brown, the sides of the head are yellowish and the crown rufous. The plumage varies according to the sub-species—the upperparts can be more or less olive-brown and the streaked underparts more or less accentuated. The nest, a bowl of leaves (bamboo, palm) lined with soft grass and rootlets, is built near the ground in low vegetation or a clump. The Striped Tit-Babbler lays three to four eggs.

87. WHITE-CRESTED LAUGHINGTHRUSH
(Garrulax leucolophus) (30 cm)

White-crested Laughingthrushes are located by their explosive song, beginning with a low murmur, immediately followed by a concert of cackling laughter taken up in a chorus by the whole group. Then, suddenly, there is silence, unless a soloist, giving the introductory signal, starts up the concert anew. With quietness falling on the forest, they can soon be seen furtively flitting about in the undergrowth. When they cross clearings they take off at intervals, one following the other, waiting to fly until the previous one is safely across in cover.

The White-crested Laughingthrush lives in small groups in evergreen and mixed forests and in bamboo, on the plain up to an altitude of 1,200 metres, but it is absent from the peninsula. The white crest and large black band over the eye distinguishes it from all the other eight laughingthrushes living in Thailand.

It feeds mainly on the ground or in low branches, pushing aside the dead leaves to find insects, seeds or fallen fruit. It also captures small reptiles and snails, breaking their shells by hammering them with its beak.

The couple builds a large bowl of roughly assembled grasses, twigs and leaves held together with pliable vegetation. The nest is placed in a bush, often at human height, sometimes higher, in a tree. The clutch varies between three and six eggs.

88. GREATER NECKLACED LAUGHINGTHRUSH
(Garrulax pectoralis) (33 cm)

The Greater Necklaced Laughingthrush frequents the undergrowth of mixed and evergreen forests from the plain up to the mountains in the west of the country. Very sociable, it lives in a group, often associated with the White-crested Laughing-thrush and the very similar Lesser Necklaced Laughingthrush *(Garrulax monileger)*. The latter, more widespread in the mainland region, is slightly smaller and is distinguished by a less marked facial pattern, that is the absence of a black moustache and streaks on the cheek. The Greater Necklaced Laughingthrush searches for its food in the ground litter of dead leaves and eats insects and small animals, as well as seeds and fruit. Loquacious, it makes varied calls including melancholic whistled notes. In the breeding period, the couple builds a nest which is placed in a bush, on a stump near the ground or several metres high. The nest is similar to that of the White-crested Laughingthrush. Three to five eggs are laid.

89. WHITE-BELLIED YUHINA
(Yuhina zantholeuca) (13 cm)

Of the four species of yuhina in Thailand, the White-bellied Yuhina is the only one to be found from the plain up to the mountains in the whole of the country. The other species are typically mountain birds and mostly limited to the northern regions.

It lives in evergreen and mixed forests, where its small shape, active amongst the leaves in a tree, can be recognised mainly by its conspicuous crest. Its plumage is not very distinctive, yellow-olive above and white below, with yellow under tail coverts.

Often in pairs, rarely in a group, the White-bellied Yuhina will join bird waves with other insectivores. Discreet, it moves nimbly in the foliage, gripping on to the end of branches in search of insects and larvae. It also eats small berries and flower nectar. Its searches are punctuated by calls of 'prrrrriit' and 'tzuit, tit-zuit'. The song is a rapid suite of 'sit, sit, sit'.

The White-bellied Yuhina makes a small cup of fibres and vegetable hair, meticulously woven, lined with leaf debris and silky matter. The nest is placed fairly low and suspended from a thin branch by threads of spiders' webs.

90. MAGPIE ROBIN *(Copsychus saularis)*   (23 cm)

The Magpie Robin is a familar sight in parks and gardens. This demonstrative bird, with its lively and jerky movements, contrasting plumage and melodious song, enlivens neighbourhoods. It brings to mind the European and American Blackbirds. It often perches in full view, tail cocked and wings drooping slightly. From dawn it bursts forth into its beautiful clear whistles. In other circumstances— flight or a skirmish with other males —it makes far less harmonious calls. The male is easily recognisable by its black and white livery. The female is greyer. The immature resembles the female except that the throat and breast are mottled with light spots. The Magpie Robin feeds largely on the ground, moving about by hopping, and eats insects, snails, worms and other prey. Its nest is a fairly loose cup of vegetable matter and sundry materials which are placed in a hole in a tree, a clump of bamboo, a crevice in a wall, under a roof or any other support which appears in connection with its life close to humans. The clutch varies between three and five eggs.

♀

♂

91. WHITE-RUMPED SHAMA
(Copsychus malabaricus)

(male 28 cm, female 22 cm)

Juvenile

An even more remarkable singer than the Magpie Robin, of which it is the forest counterpart, the White-rumped Shama is renowned for the beauty and the richness of its song. The deep melodious whistles in varying strengths and rhythms lead a good many males to little cages in the shade of a house. It lives in the thick undergrowth of evergreen forests and of mixed and secondary forests, from the plain to the middle mountain slopes. At once timid and curious, it flies off with loud angry calls if disturbed. It quickly comes to rest in a gap in the foliage which leaves it free to observe the intruder and to manifest its impatience by jerky movements of its long graduated tail. In the light of vegetable cover, the spotless white of the rump and outer tail feathers of the male contrast with the black plumage and rufous belly. The female is duller and her tail is shorter. The plumage of the immature is brown, scaled with rusty-buff above, while the throat and breast are spotted. The White-rumped Shama feeds on insects and larvae which it captures on the ground or in low bushes. It becomes more energetic in the evening and hunts actively until nightfall. During the breeding season, the couple sometimes sings in duo. The female begins a musical phrase which the male, perched above her, will continue without interruption. The coordination of the two scores is so perfect that the impression given is of one bird singing alone. The nest is a little cushion of leaves and rootlets placed in a hole in a tree fairly low down or at the base of a large bush. It contains two to four eggs.

92. STONECHAT *(Saxicola torquata)* (14 cm)

The Stonechat is principally a winter visitor in Thailand, arriving in September-October and leaving in April. It is found in open spaces, edges of cultivated and paddy fields, on the plain and high up. Isolated cases of breeding birds have been discovered in the extreme northwest of the country. It is usually by itself, perched on top of an upright twig as an observation post, from time to time giving a brief jerky flutter to its tail and wings. It pursues insects on the ground or in the air. While in Thailand, the Stonechat remains relatively silent, occasionally giving a call of alarm, 'trek, trek'. The male has black upperparts streaked with buffy-brown, orange on the breast and white patches on the neck, wings and rump. The female is duller, brown streaked with black above, buffy-brown underparts and rump and a white patch on the wing, differentiating her from the female Pied Bushchat *(Saxicola caprata)*. The immature is brown, but its breast is streaked with dark brown.

♂

93. PIED BUSCHAT (*Saxicola caprata*) (14 cm)

In Thailand, the Pied Bushchat is a resident of the open spaces, cultivated areas and scrub of the north and northeastern regions. Like the Stonechat, it perches on the end of stems of grasses and bushes, on fences and on telephone wires and eats insects which it captures on the ground and in the air.

The male is completely black, except for white patches on the wing, the rump and the tail coverts. The female is uniformly brown apart from a red rump.

Its normal alarm call is close to that of the Stonechat. During the breeding period it has a melodious warble of short repeated phrases.

The nest is a deep cup of grasses, rootlets and vegetable debris, lined with fine strands of grass and vegetable fibre. It is hidden in a shallow depression in the gound in the shelter of a clump of grass, on the side of an embankment or at the base of a bush, and contains three to five eggs.

♂

♀

94. BLUE ROCK-THRUSH *(Monticola solitarius)* (23 cm)

There are two distinct populations of the Blue Rock-Thrush in Thailand. One is a small resident population in the peninsula and the islands, and the other consists of the migrants which winter throughout the country between September and April. The birds presence is associated more with rocks and stone rather than with the surrounding vegetation, so they can also be found on the rocky outcrops in the lowland or montane forests, as well as in temple ruins or on buildings in the middle of towns. Perched on a promontary, the Blue Rock-Thrush holds itself erect, breast out, often fluttering its wings briefly. In search of food it runs in and out of the stones, hops across scattered vegetation and on the branches of bare trees. It eats insects, spiders, small reptiles and sometimes fruit and berries.

Four sub-species of the Blue Rock-Thrush have been identified in Thailand, of which *M. s. philippensis* can be clearly distinguished by the male's plumage, rufous on the belly, under the wing and the tail. The males of the other sub-species are slaty-blue, finely spotted with black and brown. The females are brown with a more or less bluish wash above and whitish with black scales below. The immature resembles the female, but is more distinctly marked on the back. The sub-species *M. s. madoci* nests locally in the rocks and cliffs. The nest, placed in a crevice, is a cup of grass, rootlets and stalks. Three eggs are laid.

Immature

95. YELLOW-BELLIED WARBLER (11 cm)
(*Abroscopus superciliaris*)

This small arboreal bird lives almost exclusively in bamboo clumps and their immediate surroundings. The Yellow-bellied Warbler is found in mixed and evergreen forests from the plain to the first foothills. It bustles about in the foliage in search of insects which it sometimes chases in short flights. Its grey head with its white eyebrow and yellow underparts distinguishes it from the other insectivores (other warblers, small flycatchers) with which it is often associated. The song is a series of six or seven fluty notes on an ascending and descending scale. The Yellow-bellied Warbler builds a small cup of vegetable fibres, moss and bamboo leaves which it places in the shelter of a dead bamboo trunk, a few metres from the ground. Three to five eggs are laid.

96. INORNATE WARBLER
(Phylloscopus inornatus)
(11 cm)

The Inornate Warbler arrives from September to winter in Thailand. Because of its small size, dull, green-olive plumage and arboreal habits, this small insectivore can easily go unnoticed. It is, however, common in all sorts of woods, from open forests to gardens, on the plain and in the mountains. There are 17 species of Leaf-warblers in Thailand. The rare features which allow differentiation between the species are usually on the upper parts of the body and thus difficult to see from the ground. They are birds that are perpetually moving about in the dense foliage and seldom allow a prolonged sighting. The Inornate Warbler has no distinguishing mark on its head, rump or tail. The wings have two yellowish bands and the tertiaries have whitish tips. It can be located by its characteristic whistle, 'wee-ist'.

97. GREAT REED-WARBLER
(Acrocephalus arundinaceus) (20 cm)

The Great Reed-Warbler breeds in Siberia, the north of China, Japan and Korea. The first birds arrive in Thailand at the end of August and the latest only leave at the end of May. During the winter, it keeps well hidden in the swampy vegetation and in bushes near the water. During migration, one can also come across them in rather drier, woody habitats. The Great Reed-Warbler moves around nimbly, climbing up and down vertical stems in search of food. It chases insects and larvae as far as the surface of the water. Occasionally it will make a brief sortie above the vegetation to snatch an insect on the wing. Opportunities for seeing it are few. Curiosity, however, sometimes persuades it to fly above the tall grasses and one can thus attract it with unusual small noises.

It can be differentiated from other aquatic warblers by its large size, uniform plumage, brown above, whitish below and narrow buffy eyebrow. Above all, the loud, harsh calls of 'kek, krak, tzek, tzek' reveal its presence and permit identification.

98. COMMON TAILORBIRD
(Orthotomus sutorius) (12 cm)

The Common Tailorbird is an inhabitant of bushy vegetation in gardens, scrub, mangroves and the edges of eroded forests. Not timid, it can often be found near houses. Constantly active, tail cocked, it threads its way with liveliness, emerging then disappearing again in the tangle of foliage in search of insects. It announces its presence with frequent ringing calls, a quick and monotonous succession of 'ti-ou'. The Common Tailorbird is olive-green above and pale below, with a rufous forecrown and traces of black on the neck. During the breeding season the male's central tail feathers grow by several centimetres. The immature birds are duller, with no mark on the forehead. It can be confused with the Dark-necked Tailorbird (*Orthotomus atrogularis*) which, although more of a forest bird, also lives in clumps in secondary vegetation where the two species can be found together. The Dark-necked Tailorbird has yellow under tail coverts and the male has a rufous head with a noticeable black patch on the neck. Tailorbirds are so named because of the ease with which they sew up leaves to shelter their nests. They join the edges of one or several leaves together with strands of vegetable fibre or spiders' webs and thread them through holes pierced by their beaks. The conical envelope thus made is lined with soft grass and vegetable down and holds three to five eggs.

♂
Nuptial

♀

130

99. TAWNY-FLANKED PRINIA *(Prinia inornata)* (15 cm)

The Tawny-flanked Prinia likes the tall grasses on the edges of swamps, cultivated and paddy fields, and grassy scrub dotted with scattered bushes. It can be found on the plain in wet areas, except in the peninsula. In twos or a small familial group, Tawny-flanked Prinias move about hidden in the vegetation, looking for insects which form their basic diet. From time to time they come out from cover to sing their energetic composition of trills and sharp notes, 'jirt-jirt-jirt-jirt'. They are not strong fliers and after a few feeble flutterings of their wings rapidly dive back into cover.

Two other prinias are very similar—the Rufescent Prinia *(Prinia rufescens)* and the Grey-breasted Prinia *(Prinia hodgsonii)*. The Tawny-flanked Prinia can be distinguished from them, with difficulty, by its call, its well marked pale eyebrow and its longer and larger tail.

Using blades of grass, down and vegetable debris, spiders' webs, the structure of the nest can take several different forms, from a deep cup hung from stems or placed in sewn up leaves, to a closed purse with a side entrance. The clutch varies between three and six eggs.

100. TICKELL'S BLUE FLYCATCHER *(Cyornis tickelliae)* (15 cm)

♂

♀

Juvenile

This small blue flycatcher lives in the evergreen and mixed forests of the plain and also frequents secondary forests and bamboo thickets. From an open perch in the undergrowth, the Tickell's Blue Flycatcher watches out for passing insects, at times moving its tail slightly. It darts out to chase them and, with a short flight, snatches its prey and returns to its perch. It readily flies about with other birds which, by their collective movements, flush out insects.
The male is a brilliant blue above and orange on the neck and breast. The female, brown above (a grey-blue wash for the sub-species in the peninsula) has a pale orange throat

and breast. They both can be distinguished from other blue flycatchers by the sharp division of colour between the breast and the belly. The immature is brown, spotted with buff. The song is composed of a soft, metallic trill of five or six notes. The nest is a small cup of rootlets and thin grasses worked into a rough mass of mosses mixed with leaves and is generally placed in a hole in a tree, but any other similar shelter can be used. Three or four eggs are laid.

101. GREY-HEADED FLYCATCHER
(Culicicapa ceylonensis) (13 cm)

The Grey-headed Flycatcher shows a preference for bushes and bamboo on the edge of small rivers. It can be found in evergreen and mixed forests, on the plain and in the mountains. A resident in the north and west of the country, as well as the peninsula, elsewhere its presence is subject to migratory and seasonal movements.

Out of the breeding season the Grey-headed Flycatcher tends to live alone but regularly joins bird waves. It actively hunts insects, hovering or darting in bold chases, at times as far as the ground. These movements are accompanied by soft whistles which have been translated as 'veni, vidi, vici', or 'silly billy'. The song is a powerful trill preceded by chirping. The adult plumage is olive-green above, grey on the head and breast and yellow on the belly. The immature is duller. The nest is a small cup of mosses and lichens, lined with fibre and held together with spiders' webs. It is placed on moss or other vegetation covering a tree trunk, stump or a rock. The female lays two to three eggs.

133

102. PIED FANTAIL *(Rhipidura javanica)* (18 cm)

The Pied Fantail lives on the plain, often near water, in the mangroves, wooded parks, gardens and secondary vegetation. It can be distinguished from the other four fantails by the large dark pectoral band above the white underparts. Constantly moving, it searches the bushes and along the small branches of trees, suddenly turning, opening and closing its tail like a fan and brushing the underside of the leaves when passing. The insects, frightened by this turbulence, are caught on the wing. These hunts are punctuated by short stanzas 'chep, chep, chep, chiwiit, chiwiit'. Aggressive with predators and intruders, the Pied Fantail does not hesitate to scold them sharply. The nest, in the shape of a cone, is made of vegetable fibre tied with spiders' webs and lined with softer material. It is placed at human height, often in a fork of a tree and extended at the base by strand of twigs. Two eggs are laid.

103. BLACK-NAPED MONARCH *(Hypothymis azurea)* (17 cm)

The Black-naped Monarch frequents the undergrowth of mixed and evergreen forests, bamboo thickets and degraded woods, from the plain up to the mountains. It is resident in Thailand and during the winter moves as far as the mangroves and into gardens. It hunts insects from a perch as well as wandering around in the foliage, from time to time fluttering its opened tail in the same way as the fantails. It makes a little hissing 'sweech-weech', whilst moving about.

Black-naped Monarchs are quite often in couples and joins in bird waves. The male is a brilliant blue with a narrow band on the breast and a black patch on the neck. The female is brown above and has a less vivid blue head. The nest is a small deep cup, more or less conical, made of vegetable fibre, bits of bark, stalks and lichen extending in strands. The whole is held together by spiders' webs and placed at variable heights in a fork or in a crossover of creepers. The clutch varies between two and four eggs.

104. ASIAN PARADISE-FLYCATCHER
(Tersiphone paradisi)

(female 21 cm, male 46 cm)

The Asian Paradise-Flycatcher is found on the plain and up to the mountains in mixed and evergreen forests, mangroves and secondary vegetation. It is both a resident and a migrant in Thailand. The male is dimorphic and has rufous or white phases. These differences in plumage and their distribution across Asia have not yet been fully explained. They may be determined by, among other things, genetic variations, membership of sub-species or the age of the bird. In India, for example, it has been noted that the male had only white plumage after its third year. This phenomenon was also observed in Indochina. The female and the immature resemble the male in its rufous stage but do not possess the two elongated central tail feathers. The Asian Paradise-Flycatcher hunts by short flights after insects, dividing its time between open undergrowth and foliage. Its resonant and rasping calls of 'chi-woeei' are a good way of identifying its presence. The nest is a vegetable cone carefully made from grasses, rootlets, fibres and bark attached by close threads of spiders' webs. It is built in the fork of a tree at various heights. Two to four eggs are laid.

105. GREY WAGTAIL *(Motacilla cinerea)* (19 cm)

The five species of wagtail found in Thailand are all winter visitors which breed in China and Russia. The first Grey Wagtails arrive in July. They can be seen everywhere near water, although their preference is for running water and open stony banks. The Grey Wagtail is rather solitary. Very alert, constantly wagging its tail, it runs up and down the river bank near the water. It flits from one stone to another, searching for insects which are its main diet and which it snatches on the wing with a brief dart. Small aquatic animals are also eaten. Its call whilst in flight is a sharp, metallic 'tsisik'.

In non-breeding plumage the adults have grey upperparts with a yellowish rump, white throat and yellow under tail. In breeding plumage, the male's throat becomes black, while that of the female remains white or has a few black spots. Like all birds, the wagtail takes particular care of its feathers which it preens meticulously. Several times throughout the day it searches with its beak and smooths down the whole length of each long feather, covering them with a fatty substance secreted by a gland under the tail.

Internuptial

137

106. RICHARD'S PIPIT *(Anthus novaeseelandiae)*   (16–20 cm)

Of the four pipits found in Thailand, the Richard's Pipit is the only breeding species. In winter, migrants arrive to augment the resident population. It is a bird common to open and cultivated areas right up to the mountains. It likes grassy scrub, stubble fields and the edge of roads. Erect on its long legs, it paces energetically up and down the flat vegetation in search of insects and sometimes seeds.

The plumage is rather dull, streaked tawny-brown and brown above. The underparts are buff with brown markings on the breast. The white edges of the outer tail feathers can be seen in flight. The immature is more streaked below. The migrant sub-species, *A. n. richardi*, is much bigger with more obvious streaks on the breast.

During mating displays, the male rises in the sky with an undulating flight, then descends in a glide, emitting a series of notes, transcribed as 'chee-wee, chee-wee'. The Richard's Pipit nests on the ground where it builds a cup of dry grasses lined with softer material, placed in the shelter of a tuft of grass. It lays three to four eggs.

138

107. ASHY WOOD-SWALLOW (*Artamus fuscus*)   (18 cm)

The Ashy Wood-Swallow is the only representative in Thailand of a bird family of Australian origin. It lives in open spaces—countryside covered with palm trees and old trees, wooded scrub, on the plain and occasionally up to the mountains. It is not found in the peninsula.
From a distance, the grey plumage appears dull. But it is finely shaded, grey-brown below with the head, wings and tail more slaty and the edge of the rump lighter. The beak is attractively bluish.
Sociable by nature, wood-swallows stay in small groups, often close together, perched on the end of a dry branch or an electric wire. From there they make brief sorties to catch insects which pass close by, often eating them on the wing. Before returning to their perch, they fly in large circles, alternating wing beats

with long glides. Whilst flying or perched, they emit their sharp, nasal call of 'mrrenk, mrrenk'.
The Ashy Wood-Swallow makes a shallow nest of grasses, roots, fibres and feathers at the top of a tree or at the base of a palm leaf, in which it lays two to three eggs. It will firmly chase away crows, raptors and other kidnapping birds as soon as they approach its nest.

108. BROWN SHRIKE *(Lanius cristatus)* (19 cm)

The Brown Shrike is a very common winter visitor in Thailand from August to April. It frequents the open spaces of the plain to the mountains, countryside, secondary vegetation, the clearings in dry forests and bushes. It is usually seen alone, perched on the top of a bush, an electric wire or an upright stem. It hunts by lying in wait and seizing its prey on the ground, eating large insects and small vertebrates. It often announces itself with a resonant 'chek, ek, ek, ek'. Depending on the sub-species, the plumage varies slightly. Upperparts are grey-brown to rufous-brown and a large black band overlined by a white eyebrow covers the face. The crown and tail are often more rufous than the back. The underparts are white tinged with buff. The immature is duller, the body almost entirely barred with blackish lines.

109. LONG-TAILED SHRIKE *(Lanius schach)* (25 cm)

Of the five species of shrikes occuring in Thailand, two are resident, the Long-tailed Shrike in the mainland region, and the Burmese Shrike (*Lanius collurioides*) which breeds locally in the mountains of the northwest and winters in the continental plains. The Long-tailed Shrike frequents open areas, cultivated countryside and bushy scrub right up to the mountains. Often perched conspicuously, it can be seen easily. However, like other shrikes, it remains unobtrusive at certain times of the year, staying hidden in the vegetation. It hunts by lying in wait for all sorts of small animal prey, which it does not always eat immediately but hoards by impaling them on thorns, forming a larder. This habit, common amongst shrikes, seems to be limited to the breeding season. The plumage is elegant and contrasted. The head, wings and long tail are black, the back is bright rufous and the underparts are white. The flanks and sides of the body are light rufous. In flight, the two white spots on the wing are particularly noticeable. The immature birds, duller than the adults, have the side of the body streaked. The very similar Burmese Shrike has grey on the head and top of the back, chestnut upperparts and a shorter, black tail with a white border. The alarm calls of the Long-tailed Shrike, hoarse and sharp, are as unmusical as other shrikes. Its song is reputed to be melodious and it is said to be capable of remarkable mimicry.

The nest is a fairly large and deep cup made up of different materials (branches, roots and stems) and lined with soft grass and rootlets. It is usually placed several metres up in a thick or thorny bush. The clutch varies between four and six eggs.

110. ASIAN PIED STARLING *(Sturnus contra)* (24 cm)

The Asian Pied Starling can be found in small groups in open countryside, in the vicinity of paddy fields and swamps, in grassland and scrub. A resident of the plain except in the peninsula, it can be identified by its black and white livery which contrasts with its yellow beak. In the immature, the black is replaced by brown.

The Asian Pied Starling feeds on the ground, hurriedly scurrying in the low vegetation here and there pecking at insects. Then, it flies off to perch a little further away and carries on prospecting, regularly looking around with a nervous movement of its head to survey its surroundings. It also eats fruit and seeds.

At night, Asian Pied Starlings gather in a tree with other starlings, forming noisy dormitories. Their repertoire is varied and they mix melodious and clear notes with harsh and discordant sounds. Built at the top of a tree, the nest is a voluminous dome of roughly assembled stalks, grasses and leaves placed on a platform of twigs. It generally contains five eggs.

Juvenile

Adult

111. BLACK-COLLARED STARLING *(Sturnus nigricollis)* (28 cm)

The Black-collared Starling can be found everywhere in Thailand as far as the middle slopes of the mountains. Today it is progressively but sporadically settling in the peninsula, from which it was absent a few decades ago.

It can be distinguished from the Asian Pied Starling by its large size, heavier shape and lighter plumage. The black neck collar separates the whitish head and throat from the grey-brown back. In flight, its white rump and tail tip can be clearly seen. The immature does not have a black collar, and its upperparts are brown whereas the head, neck and breast

are grey, finely streaked with white. As sociable as other starlings, the Black-collared Starling lives near villages, secondary vegetation and cultivated areas. It eats mainly insects which it captures during its wanderings.

Its vocalisations are varied—liquid notes that sound like 'chir, chu, chu' and 'chir, ta, chou, ta, chou' can often be heard. It builds a dome of grasses, twigs and varied materials, similar to that of the Asian Pied Starling, which it places high up in a palm or other large tree. Several nests are sometimes found close together. The clutch is generally four eggs.

143

112. COMMON MYNA
(Acridotheres tristis)   (25 cm)

A native of India, Burma and China, the Common Myna started its rapid and effective advance into Thailand at the beginning of the century. In the 1920s it was already abundant more or less everywhere and its area of distribution rapidly spread to the peninsula, then Malaysia. Its Latin name, probably attributed to its plumage, is highly inappropriate given its lively and cheeky character. Its appearance is well-known, brown and black enhanced by a bright yellow lappet on the eye. The beak and feet are yellow. In flight, a white patch on the wings and white tail tips can be seen. It seldom leaves areas inhabited by humans and can be seen on lawns in suburbs, villages and in the countryside. Often in twos, the Common Mynas pace up and down open spaces with a distinctive gait, bobbing their heads at each step. Omnivorous, they eat insects and worms, fruit and scraps. They are also partial to flower nectar.

The voice of the Common Myna is a mixture of raucous and ventriloquial sounds and liquid notes, 'kiky, kiky, kiky, chour, chour, kok, kok, kok'. Living near humans leads it to nest on buildings and structures, in holes and under roofs. It also uses holes in trees and the top of palm trees, where it piles up twigs, straw, stalks and feathers, forming a rough nest in which it lays three to six eggs.
In the cultivated land and open forests of the peninsula, a similar species, the Jungle Myna (*Acridotheres fuscus*) can be seen although it is less widespread. Its plumage is dark brown shaded with grey, and its head is black with no yellow lappet on the eye. It has a short crest on the front of the forehead, which is difficult to see from a distance.

113. WHITE-VENTED MYNA
(Acridotheres javanicus)   (25 cm)

Further from humans, the White-vented Myna prefers open countryside and cultivated areas, with the exception of the peninsula. Up to the beginning of the 1980s there was a large dormitory of White-vented Mynas in the station of Hua Lampong in Bangkok. In the evening, hundreds of birds gathered on the metal girders of the building in a racket of calls and chatterings. These were probably chased away when the repairs and cleaning of the building were carried out.
The White-vented Myna is found near cattle, where it is able to catch insects hidden in the grass which

have been disturbed by the movement of the animals. Sometimes it perches on their backs and rids them of parasites.

Perched, it appears all black with the exception of the belly, under tail feathers, white under wings and yellow beak and legs. A tuft of feathers on the forehead forms a small crest. The immature birds are browner. Its flight is straight and fast with vigorous wing beats, showing the white marks on the wings and the tip of the tail. The voice is very similar to that of the Common Myna. It nests in holes in trees or at the top of palm trees and builds a structure of twigs, straw and feathers in which it lays two to six eggs.

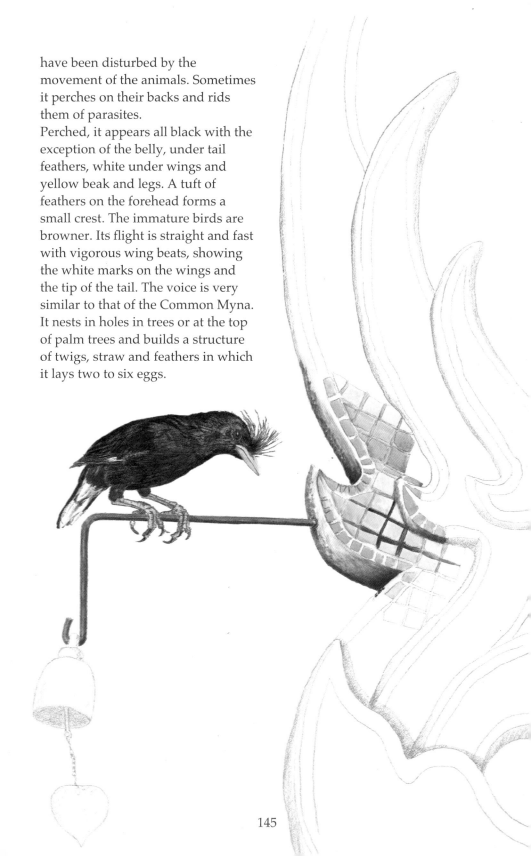

114. HILL MYNA (*Gracula religiosa*) (30 cm)

The Hill Myna is famous throughout the world for its ability to imitate the human voice. Its popularity as a cage bird endangers a species once widespread in Thailand and which today is rarely seen outside parks and nature reserves.

It is a forest bird, typically arboreal, which lives as far as the mountains, except in the peninsula where it stays in the plain. Sociable by nature, it moves around in small groups eating mainly fruit. It also eats insects and other small animals as well as nectar from certain flowers.

From its glossy plumage, two well developed yellow lappets stand out on the side of the head. The beak is orange and the feet yellow. A large white patch on the wing is particularly visible in flight.

Its vocal repertoire is varied and unexpected. One can sometimes hear a mixture of groans, whistles, chuckles and strange calls. However, its most distinctive call, often uttered at the top of a dead tree, is a powerful whistle, 'ti-ong', which rings out especially in the morning and evening. On the other hand, however gifted it might be at learning sounds whilst in captivity, it cannot imitate the songs of other birds.

The Hill Myna nests in a hole in a tree, usually high up, and lays two to three eggs. It is said that couples pair for life and that the same nest site is reused each year.

146

115. OLIVE-BACKED SUNBIRD
(Nectarinia jugularis) (11 cm)

The Olive-backed Sunbird is common everywhere in Thailand, on the plain, in parks and gardens, open woodlands, secondary vegetation and mangroves. The plumage of the male is adorned with a metallic violet-blue on the forehead, throat and top of the breast, contrasting with the vivid yellow on the belly. After the breeding season, the dark colouring is reduced to a central band in the male's eclipse plumage, and to a few spots on the immature's throat. The sides of the chest have orange tufts, often hidden by the wings. The female is yellow below and olive-brown above. The edges of the outer wing feathers are white.

The Olive-backed Sunbird flits from one flower to another in the trees and bushes, feeding on nectar. Perched near, or directly on the corolla, it takes up the sap from the flowers with its tubular tongue and sometimes pierces the base of the calyx with its thin, curved beak to reach its food. It also eats small insects attracted by the flowers. Its call is a resonant and rising 'sweet'. At first sight the nest, in the form of a purse, resembles a mass of debris rather than an elaborate structure. It is made up of grass and fibres tied up with spiders' webs and trimmed with mosses, lichens and bark. The entrance on the side is protected by a small roof. It is hung, several metres high, on a branch, sometimes in unexpected places such as telephone wires or awnings. Two eggs are usually laid.

♂

Immature

♀

147

116. SCARLET-BACKED FLOWERPECKER (9 cm)
(*Dicaeum cruentatum*)

Very small and stocky, the Scarlet-backed Flowerpecker is common in orchards around villages and in parks in towns. It also lives on the edges of deciduous and mixed woods and in secondary vegetation. The male has a large scarlet band from the head to the rump. The sides of the head, the wings and the tail are black and the front is whitish. The female is duller with only a red rump. The immature has no bright colouring, apart from an orange spot at the base of the beak. The Scarlet-backed Flowerpecker moves about rapidly, making its sharp, jerky calls of 'tchik, tchik'. It moves around at the top of trees and high branches, where it feeds on insects, spiders, nectar from flowers and berries. Flowerpeckers probably play an important part in the propagation of certain parasitical plants, particularly the loranthus to which the Scarlet-backed Flowerpecker is especially partial. Before eating the gelatinous berries, it will rub them lightly along the bark of a branch. The nest is a small silky structure in the shape of an egg, made of vegetable down and fibres and carefully assembled with the aid of spiders' webs. Often hidden by the leaves, it is hung at the end of a branch and contains two to three eggs.

♂

117. ORIENTAL WHITE-EYE *(Zosterops palpebrosa)* (11 cm)

Of the four species of white-eye in Thailand, the Oriental White-Eye is the most widespread. It frequents all types of forest, from the plain to the mountains and can also be seen in mangroves, open woodlands and gardens.

Remarkable for the large white circle surrounging the eye, the different white-eyes are relatively difficult to distinguish in the wild. The Oriental White-Eye has a narow yellow band on the front of its forehead and a largish yellow stripe separates the lower breast and grey belly, the rest of the underparts being yellow. In the west of the country, numerous birds have all their underparts completely yellow.

They move around in small groups, accompanying their movements with feeble cheepings. They take possession of a tree or a bush, inspecting the foliage and flower corollas to chase out insects and spiders or to lap up the nectar. Just as readily they eat buds, berries and fruit. Then they fly off one after the other, leaving as quickly as they came.

The song of the Oriental White-Eye is a short melody, at first nearly inaudible and slowly getting louder. To nest, it builds a cup of thin grass, rootlets and moss which it hangs in a small fork at the end of a branch. Two to four eggs are laid.

117

116

♀

149

118. LITTLE SPIDERHUNTER
(Arachnothera longirostra) (16 cm)

The Little Spiderhunter is stockier than the sunbird and it has a much more imposing beak. It lives in the undergrowth of mixed and evergreen forests and in wooded secondary vegetation and has a particular liking for ginger and banana plants in humid gullies. It is the smallest of the seven spiderhunters found in Thailand. Upperparts are olive-brown, underparts yellow and the throat whitish. The orange pectoral tufts are hardly visible. Always active, it moves about quickly and it is not easy to get a good sighting. It eats nectar from flowers, particularly from bananas, thus contributing to pollination. It also eats insects and spiders which it catches by hovering in front of their webs.

It is often noticed by its call, a repetitious sharp 'chip, chip, chip'. The nest is a structure of grasses, dried leaves, fibres and vegetable down, held up by more rigid elements and sewn with spiders' webs to the underside of a large leaf. The entrance is at the side. Two to three eggs are laid.

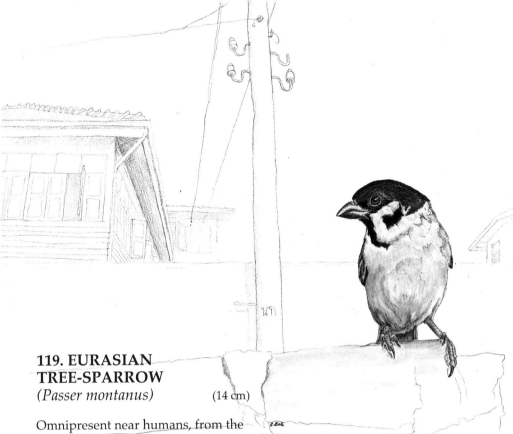

119. EURASIAN TREE-SPARROW
(Passer montanus) (14 cm)

Omnipresent near humans, from the megalopolis of Bangkok to the smallest villages, the Eurasian Tree-Sparrow is without a doubt the first bird one comes across. It is found everywhere in inhabited zones, as far as the limits of human settlements. The male and female are identical—a chestnut crown, a black patch on the white sides of the head and a black bib. The plumage of the immature is less vivid, in particular on the crown and cheeks. The Eurasian Tree-Sparrow eats seeds, insects and kitchen left-overs. Its nest, made of straw and twigs, lined with feathers, can be found in holes, crevices and under roofs. The clutch varies between four and six eggs. Preferring scattered woodland and cultivation near villages, the Plain-backed Sparrow (*Passer flaveolus*) seems, in comparison, to be the country sparrow. Its plumage is more coloured than that of the Eurasian Tree-Sparrow and shows sexual dimorphism. The male is grey-green and chestnut above and pale yellow below with a black bib. The female has uniformly beige upperparts, well marked with a light eyebrow and yellowish underparts.

A third species, the House Sparrow (*Passer domesticus*), has recently made its appearance in the north of Thailand and could well start a larger colony. The male has a grey crown and a large black bib, the female is streaked with no distinctive mark on the head except a pale eyebrow.

120. WHITE-RUMPED MUNIA (*Lonchura striata*) (12 cm)

The White-rumped Munia is common in cultivated land and scrub. It can also be seen far from fields, in dry and scattered forests up to the mountains. The adult is a finely streaked dark brown on its back, throat and top of the breast. The creamy belly is lightly spotted with brown and the rump is white with a blackish tapered tail. The immature is paler. Munias feed in small groups, pecking from the ground or climbing along stalks to pick off the seeds from the grassy plants, cereals and bamboo. A soft call of 'prrrit', is frequently heard. The nest of the White-rumped Munia is a ball of grasses and leaves, not looking very neat, with an entrance on the side. Placed in a bush, at the end of a branch or in a palm tree, it contains three to eight eggs.

121. SCALY-BREASTED MUNIA *(Lonchura punctulata)* (12 cm)

Similar in behaviour to the White-rumped Munia, the Scaly-breasted Munia is distinguished by its paler brown colouring and the absence of white on the rump. The immature is brown above and buff below, and the beak is dark grey.

The Scaly-breasted Munia lives in cultivated land, paddy fields and grassy scrub up to the middle mountain slopes. It hardly ever goes into wooded areas. As harvest time approaches, attracted by the ripe grain, groups of munias invade the rice fields to feed, to the exasperation of the farmers. Here and there on the small plots picturesque bird scaring systems, for instance, a network of strings stretched across the fields to which tin cans have been attached, can still be seen. Pulling one end of the string makes the tins clatter, frightening off the birds.

The nest of the Scaly-breasted Munia is similar to that of the White-rumped Munia—a round structure made of grasses and twigs, placed in a bush or a palm tree. The clutch varies from five to seven eggs.

Immature

Adult

153

122. BAYA WEAVER (*Ploceus philippinus*) (15 cm)

The Baya Weaver can be seen by chance in the countryside and on the plain as far as the middle mountain slopes. Its thick conical beak immediately reveals it as a grain eater. It eats grain from wild plants as well as cultivated ones, particularly rice. During the breeding season it also captures insects which it feeds its young. In breeding plumage, the male acquires a bright yellow cap and a black band on the eye. Underparts are a uniform buff. In non-breeding plumage it resembles the female, tawny-buff below and buff streaked with brown on the back. It is only distinguished from the Asian Golden Weaver (*Ploceus hypoxanthus*) by the lighter shade of the parts uniformly coloured and the rather less solid beak. The Asian Golden Weaver is confined to the central region, and during the breeding season the male is bright yellow except on the back, wings and tail, with a black face and throat. The breeding habits of the Baya Weaver are singular. It nests in a small colony in trees, hanging its globular nest from a branch. This impressive, finely woven, structure of grasses comprises one round room extended at the bottom by a long access tunnel. The male alone builds the nest, after which it struts around to attract a female. At first, he builds a rough shape of the top half with a large space in the side. The female comes to inspect and test the soundness of the structure before agreeing to mate. The male then quickly finishes the nest and the female installs herself to lay, hatch and bring up the young alone. The male, being polygamous, goes through the same motions again in order to attract other females.

♂
Nuptial

154

123. CRESTED BUNTING *(Melophus lathami)* (16 cm)

Like all the buntings seen in Thailand, the Crested Bunting is a winter visitor. It breeds to the northeast of Indochina and China, to the west Burma and India. During the winter it can be seen in the north, where it shows a preference for hilly terrain, grassy scrub and higher cultivated areas. Often in a small group, mixed with other buntings, the Crested Bunting eats seeds and other vegetation from the ground. It often takes refuge readily on rocky outcrops or in low bushes.

The black and rufous plumage of the male is particularly distinctive. In winter, the edges of the black feathers become scaled with greeny-brown, toning down the bright contrast of the breeding plumage. The female is duller, with a less prominent crest, browny-green streaked with black above and dark brown buff underneath with vague streaks on the flanks and breast. The outer tail feathers and wing edges are rufous.

♂
Internuptial

155

Further Reading

This book is an invitation to extend research and investigation further, and growing curiosity will lead the reader to turn to more complete works.

- **Identification Guides**

   Lekagul,B. ; Round, P. R. ; Wongkalasin, M. ; Komolphalin, K. *A Guide to the Birds of Thailand.*
   Saha Karn Bhaet, Bangkok (1991). This book describes all the species, specifying their distribution,status and their habitat.
   King, B. ; Dickson, E. C. ; Woodcock, M. W. *A Field Guide to the Birds of South East Asia.* Collins, London (1975). This book will provide information on the identification and distribution of birds in Southeast Asia.

- **Guides for Naturalists**

   South-east Asia Wildlife. Apa Publications (Insight Guides), Hong Kong (1991)
   Taylor, K. A. *A Birders Guide to Thailand* (1993)
   Gray, Piprell and Graham. *National Parks of Thailand.* Revised edition. Bangkok (1994).

- **Guide Books to National Parks**

   Birds of Doi Inthanon National Park : check-list and guide to bird finding (1989)
   Birds of Khao Yai National Park : check-list and site guide (1989)
   Birds of Khao Sam RoiYot National Park : check-list and guide to bird finding (1993)
   Centre for Conservation Biology, Faculty of Science, Mahidol University, Bangkok.

- **Radio cassette**

   The calls and songs are an important element in the location and identification of birds. A partial collection on cassette (138 species of South-East Asia), made by T White, *A Field Guide to the Bird Songs of South-East Asia*, available from the British Library National Sound Archive, 29 Exhibition Road, London SW7 2AS, Great Britain.

USEFUL ADDRESSES

- **The Royal Forestry Department** is responsible for the management of forests and nature conservation in Thailand. Information concerning access to protected sites can be obtained from: 61, Paholyothin Road, Bangkren, Bangkok 10900

- **The Bird Conservation Society** is an active association for the promotion of ornithology in Thailand. It organises regular meetings, field trips and publishes a monthly bulletin.
  P. O Box13, Ratchathevi Post Office, Bangkok 10401

- **Centre for Wildlife Research**, based at the Faculty of Science's Department of Biology at Mahidol, centralises all ecological information on a data bank with the aim of promoting the conservation of the environment and animals species.
  Faculty of Science, Mahidol University, Rama VI Road, Bangkok 10400.

- **Wildlife Fund Thailand (WFT)**
  255 Soi Asoke, Sukhumvit 21, Bangkok 10110

- **World Wildlife Fund for Nature (WWF) Thailand**
  AT 104 Outreach, PO Box 2751, Bangkok 10501

- The Natural History section of the **Siam Society** publishes a scientific journal, *The Natural History Bulletin of the Siam Society*, twice a year. It contains articles on natural history, including birds.
  131 Soi Asoke, Sukhumvit Road Bangkok

- **The Oriental Bird Club**, based in the United Kingdom, aims to gather information on the birds of the entire Asian region. It publishes a bulletin and a journal, *Forktail*. One can join by contacting: c/o the Lodge, Sandy, Bedfordshire Sgl9 2DL (Great Britain)

Where to See Birds in Thailand

The network of protected areas comprises about 77 national parks and about 50 forest parks, 30 wildlife sanctuaries and about 30 non-hunting areas.

National parks are open to the public and are popular recreation sites for the people of Thailand. However, their ecological and ornithological interests are uneven. The sanctuaries and reserves were created with the primary objective of conserving a habitat for one or several species. They are not organised for tourists though it is possible to pay a short visit.

To obtain more information on access and accommodation it is advisable to contact the **Royal Forest Department** and the **National Parks Division** of the Royal Forest Department which issues passes.

Below, we suggest a few places, with relatively easy access, in which to see birds in Thailand. (The nearest town is in brackets).

NORTH
Chiang Saen (Chiang Rai) - Located near the Mekong River, Chiang Saen is a cultivated area including lakes which offers a good opportunity to see wintering birds.
Doi Inthanon (Chom Thong) - With the highest summit in Thailand (2,590 metres), this national park supports a large variety of species, from the dry diterocarp up to the evergreen forests.
Doi Suthep-Pui (Chiang Mai) - Very close to Chiang Mai and therefore touristy, but hosts a variety of montane forest birds.
Doi Khun Tan (Lampang) - A national park with picturesque access by train on the Chiang Mai-Lampang line. A signposted path leads to the summit at 1,375 metres, crossing dry dipterocarp forest in the plain up to hill evergreen forest, scattered with pines.
Doi Chiang Dao (Chiang Dao) - This sanctuary shelters the rare and endemic Deignan's Babbler, as well as other montane birds of hill evergreen forests.

NORTHEAST
Khao Yai (Pak Chong) - The oldest (1962) and best known of the national parks, Khao Yai has a fauna as rich in birds as it does in mammals.
Nam Nao (Lom Sak) - This park offers a variety of forest types (deciduous, mixed, evergreen, and conifers) and the birds associated with them.

WEST
Khao Sam Roi Yot (Pran Buri) - Situated near the sea, this park includes a large fresh water swamp, beaches and mudflats favourable to waterfowl and shore birds.
Kaeng Krachan (Petchaburi) - The largest of the national parks in Thailand, Kaeng Krachan has an artificial lake near the Park House. Primary evergreen forests offer

good opportunities for observation.

Huai Kha Kaeng (Uthai Tani) - This wildlife sanctuary encompasses large areas of lowland deciduous forest and with the Thung Yai reserve nearby constitutes one of the richest sites in Thailand for the conservation of large mammals and birds.

PENINSULA

Thale Ban (Satun) - This park is an example of a rain forest and most of the peninsular forest species can be seen here.

Khao Luang (Nakhon Si Thammarat) - This park shelters an array of montane and sub-montane rain forest birds.

Thalae Noi (Pattalung) - This game reserve is a large fresh water lake and shelters resident and wintering waterfowl and alrger water birds.

Ko Libong (accessible by boat from Kantang) This reserve is an exceptional site to watch wintering and passing shorebirds, including the rarer ones.

Khao Pra Bang Khram (Krabi) - This game reserve is of particular interest for lowland rain forest birds.

SOUTHEAST

Khao Soi Dao (Chantaburi) - This is an important site for Indochinese montane birds.

CENTRAL

Bung Borapet (Pitsanulok) - This game reserve, a large wetland including an artificial lake and marshy areas, is a refuge for breeding and wintering water birds.

Ban Lung Tua (Pitsanulok) - This reserve is a small pond in cultivated land where a number of waterfowl winter.

Wat Phai Lom (Pathum Thani) - A temple reserve sheltering an important colony of Asian Openbills of several thousand nests. The surrounding countryside is good for observation of birds in the field.

The intertidal mudflats and salt marshes on the coast of Thailand, particularly at **Bangpoo, Samut Sakorn and Samut Sonkran,** are excellent sites to watch wintering or passing shorebirds.

Glossary

Aquatic:	water living e.g. ducks, grebes
Arboreal:	tree-living
Arthropods:	member of Arthropoda, a division of animal kingdom with segmented bodies - crustacea, millipedes, insects, arachnids
Biotope:	habitat of plant or animal life
Cap:	usually used to denote a larger area than the crown i.e., the forehead, crown, upper nape, and eyebrow area combined
Casque:	an enlargement of the upper part of the bill, e.g. on hornbills
Dimorphism:	the occurrence of two forms in the same species
Endemic:	indigenous. SE Asia has 44 endemic bird species
Epiphyte:	a plant growing on another plant without being parasitic
Face:	the lores, orbital area, forepart of cheeks and malar area combined
Gastropods:	any member of the Gastropoda, a class of asymmetrical molluscs in which the foot is broad and flat, the mantle undivided, the shell in one piece usually conical, e.g. limpets, whelks, snails, slugs
Hackles:	long slender feathers found on neck of Red Junglefowl, Nicobar Pigeon
Head:	forehead, crown, nape and sides of head combined
Immature:	used to denote all plumage phases except the adult plumage and a few subadult plumages
Lappet:	a fold of skin hanging from the head
Lophophore:	Crested gallinaceous bird
Malar area:	the area bounded by the base of the bill, the sides of the throat and lower corner of the eye.
Mantle:	the back, upper wing coverts and scapulars combined
Morphology:	science of form, especially that of the outer form, inner structure and development of living organisms and their parts
Oscines:	song birds, forming main body of the Passeriformes
Palaearctic:	North Africa (including the Sahara) Greenland and Eurasia (except southern Arabia, the area south of the Himalayas, southern China and SE Asia
Passeriformes:	the order of perching birds
Photoperiod:	optimum length of day, as it affects the amount of light received by plants or animals for their normal growth and development
Procrypsis:	protective colouration
Raptor:	bird of prey
Terrestrial:	ground-living
Underparts:	undersurface of body from throat to under tail coverts
Upperparts:	upper surface of body; includes the upper surface of the wings and tail; also includes the head unless otherwise stated or implied.
Vinaceous:	wine coloured
Wattle:	a piece of bare skin, often brightly coloured, usually hanging from some part of the head or neck.

<u>Illustrations</u>
Internuptial=Non-breeding. Plumage acquired after the breeding season is usually duller than breeding plumage.
Nuptial=Breeding

Complete list of the Birds of Thailand

This list follows the systematic order of the **Field Guide of the Birds of South-East Asia** (King et al,1975). The scientific names are those used by Lekagul and Round in **A Guide to the Birds of Thailand** (1991)

DEFINITION OF STATUS TERMS

R: resident
V: migrant, winter visitor or passing through
A: accidental, rare visitor to Thailand
E: extinct, disappeared from Thailand
N: breeder, only in Thailand for breeding
R & V: population of residents and migrants
?: indicates that status has not been precisely defined
*: species mentioned in this book

Podicipedidae : GREBES
1. Little Grebe (*Tachybaptus ruficollis) R*
2. Great Crested Grebe (*Podiceps cristatus*) A

Procellariidae : SHEARWATERS
3. Streaked Shearwater (*Calonectris leucomelas*) A
4. Short-tailed Shearwater (*Puffinus tenuirostris*) A

Hydrobatidae : STORM-PETRELS
5. Swinhoe's Storm-Petrel (*Oceanodroma monorhis*) V

Phaethondidae : TROPICBIRDS
6. White-tailed Tropicbird (*Phaeton lepturus*) V

Pelecanidae : PELICANS
7. Spot-billed Pelican (*Pelecanus philippensis*) V

Sulidae : BOOBIES
8. Masked Booby (*Sula dactylatra*) A
9. Brown Booby *(Sula leucogaster)* V

Phalacrocoracidae : CORMORANTS
10. Great Cormorant (*Phalacrocorax carbo*) V
11. Indian Shag (*Phalacrocorax fusicollis*) R
12. Little Cormorant (*Phalacrocorax niger*) R *

Anhingidae : DARTERS
13. Oriental Darter (*Anhinga melanogaster*) R ?

Fregatidae : FRIGATEBIRDS
14. Christmas Frigatebird (*Fregata andrewsi*) V
15. Great Frigatebird (*Fregata minor*) V
16. Lesser Frigatebird (*Fregata ariel*) V

Ardeidae : HERONS, EGRETS, BITTERNS
17. Great-Billed Heron (*Ardea sumatrana*) R
18. Grey Heron (*Ardea cinerea*) V
19. Purple Heron (*Ardea purpurea*) R & V
20. Little Heron (*Butorides striatus*) R & V *
21. Javan Pond-Heron (*Ardeola speciosa*) R *
22. Chinese Pond-Heron (*Ardeola bacchus*) V *
23. Cattle Egret (*Bubulcus ibis*) R *
24. Pacific Reef Egret (*Egretta sacra*) R
25. Chinese Egret (*Egretta eulophotes*) R
26. Great Egret (*Egretta alba*) R & V *
27. Plumed Egret (*Egretta intermedia*) V *
28. Little Egret (*Egretta garzetta*) R & V *
29. Black-crowned Night-Heron (*Nycticorax nycticorax*) R & V
30. Malayan Night-Heron (*Gorsachius melanolophus*) R & V
31. Yellow Bittern (*Ixobrychus sinensis*) R & V
32. Schrenk's Bittern (*Ixobrychus eurythmus*) V
33. Cinnamon Bittern (*Ixobrychus*

cinnamomeus) R
34. Black Bittern (*Dupetor flavicollis*) N & V
35. Great Bittern (*Botaurus stellaris*) V

Ciconiidae : STORKS
36. Painted Stork (*Mycteria leucocephala*) N & V
37. Milky Stork (*Mycteria cinerea*) E ?
38. Asian Openbill (*Anastomus oscitans*) N *
39. White Stork (*Ciconia ciconia*) A
40. Black Stork (*Ciconia nigra*) V
41. Woolly-necked Stork (*Ciconia episcopus*) R
42. Storm's Stork (*Ciconia stormi*) R
43. Black-necked Stork (*Ephippiorhynchus asiaticus*) ? R
44. Greater Adjutant (*Leptopilos dubius*) V
45. Lesser Adjutant (*Leptopilos javanicus*) R & V

Threskiornithidae : IBIS, SPOONBILLS
46. Black-headed Ibis (*Threskiornis melanocephalus*) V
47. White-shouldered Ibis (*Pseudibis davisoni*) E
48. Giant Ibis (*Pseudibis gigantea*) E.
49. Glossy Ibis (*Plegadis falcinellus*) A
50. Black-faced Spoonbill (*Platalea minor*) A
51. White Spoonbill (*Platalea leucoradia*) A

Anatidae : GEESE, DUCKS
52. Bar-headed Goose (*Anser indicus*) A
53. Lesser Treeduck (*Dendrocygna javanica*) R & V *
54. Ruddy Shellduck (*Tadorna ferruginea*) V
55. Common Shellduck (*Tadorna tadorna*) A
56. Common Pintail (*Anas acuta*) V
57. Baikal Teal (*Anas formosa*) A
58. Common Teal (*Anas crecca*) V
59 Spot-billed Duck (*Anas poecilorhyncha*) V
60. Gadwall (*Anas strepera*) A
61. Eurasian Wigeon (*Anas penelope*) V
62. Garganey (*Anas querquedula*) V
63. Northern Shoveller (*Anas clypeata*) V
64. Falcated Teal (*Anas falcata*) V
65. Mallard (*Anas platyrhynchos*) A
66. Red-crested Pochard (*Netta rufina*) A
67. Common Pochard (*Aythya ferina*) A
68 White-eyed Pochard (*Aythya nyroca*) V
69. Baer's Pochard (*Aythya baeri*) A
70. Tufted Duck (*Aythya fuligula*) V
71. Mandarin Duck (*Aix galericulata*) A
72. Cotton Pygmy Goose (*Nettapus coromandelianus*) R
73.Comb Duck (*Sarkidiornis melanotos*) R? & V
74. White-winged Duck (*Cairina scutulata*) R

Pandionidae : OSPREY
75. Osprey (*Pandion haliaetus*) V

Accipitridae : KITES, HAWKS, EAGLES, VULTURES
76. Jerdon's Baza (*Aviceda jerdoni*) R & V
77. Black Baza (*Aviceda leuphotes*) R & V
78. Eurasian HoneyBuzzard (*Pernis ptilorhynchus*) R & V
79. Black-shouldered Kite (*Elanus caeruleus*) R*
80. Black Kite (*Milvus migrans*) R & V *
81. Brahminy Kite (*Haliastur indus*) R *
82. White-bellied Sea-Eagle (*Haliaeetus leucogaster*) R
83. Pallas's Fish-Eagle (*Haliaeetus leucoryphus*)A
84. White-tailed Eagle (*Haliaeetus albicilla*) A
85. Fish Eagle (*Icthyophaga humilis*) R
86. Grey-headed Fish-Eagle (*Ichthyophaga ichthyaetus*) R
87. White-rumped Vulture (*Gyps bengalensis*) R? & V
88. Long-billed Vulture (*Gyps indicus*) E?
89. Cinereous Vulture (*Aegypius monachus*) V
90. Red-headed Vulture (*Sarcogyps calvus*) R
91. Short-toed Eagle (*Circaetus gallicus*) V
92. Crested Serpent Eagle (*Spilornis cheela*) R *
93. Eastern Marsh Harrier (*Circus spilonotus*) V
94. Northern Harrier (*Circus cyaneus*) V
95. Pied Harrier (*Circus melanoleucos*) V
96. Northern Goshawk (*Accipiter gentilis*) V
97. Besra (*Accipiter virgatus*) R
98. Japanese Sparrowhawk (*Accipiter gularis*) V
99. Northern Sparrowhawk (*Accipiter nisus*) V
100. Crested Goshawk (*Accipiter trivirgatus*) R
101. Chinese Goshawk (*Accipiter soloensis*) V
102. Shikra (*Accipiter badius*) R *
103. Rufous-winged Buzzard (*Butastur liventer*) R
104. Grey-faced Buzzard (*Butastur indicus*) V
105. Common Buzzard (*Buteo buteo*) V
106. Black Eagle (*Ictinaetus malayensis*) R *
107. Greater Spotted Eagle (*Aquila clanga*) V
108. Tawny Eagle (*Aquila rapax*) A
109. Imperial Eagle (*Aquila heliaca*) V
110. Bonelli's Eagle (*Hieraaetus fasciatus*) R?
111. Booted Eagle (*Hieraaetus pennatus*) V
112. Rufous-bellied Eagle (*Hieraaetus kienerii*) R
113. Changeable Hawk-Eagle (*Spizaetus cirrhatus*) R *
114. Mountain Hawk-Eagle (*Spizaetus nipalensis*) R
115. Blyth's Hawk-Eagle (*Spizaetus alboniger*) R
116. Wallace's Hawk-Eagle (*Spizaetus nanus*) R

Falconidae : FALCONS
117. White-rumped Falcon (*Polihierax insignis*)
R
118. Collared Falconet (*Microhierax caerulescens*) R
119. Black-thighed Falconet (*Microhierax fringillarius*) R
120. Eurasian Kestrel (*Falco tinnunculus*) V
121. Amur Falcon (*Falco amurensis*) A
122. Northern Hobby (*Falco subbuteo*) V
123. Oriental Hobby (*Falco severus*) R
124. Peregrine Falcon (*Falco peregrinus*) R & V
125. Bat Hawk (*Macheirhamphus alcinus*) R

Phasianidae : QUAILS, PARTRIDGE, PHEASANTS
126. Chinese Francolin (*Francolinus pintadeanus*) R
127. Long-billed Partridge (*Rhizothera longirostris*) R
128. Japanese Quail (*Coturnix japonica*) A
129. Rain Quail (*Coturnix coromandelica*) R
130. Blue-breasted Quail (*Coturnix chinensis*) R
131. Common Hill-Partridge (*Arborophila rufogularis*) R
132. Bar-backed Partridge (*Arborophila brunneopectus*) R
133. Chestnut-headed Partridge (*Arborophila cambodiana*) R
134. Scaly-breasted Partridge (*Arborophila chloropus*) R
135. Chestnut-necklaced Partridge (*Arborophila charltoni*) R?
136. Ferruginous Wood-Partridge (*Caloperdrix oculea*) R
137. Crested Wood-Partridge (*Rollulus rouloul*) R
138. Mountain Bamboo Partridge (*Bambusicola fytchii*) R
139. Kalij Pheasant (*Lophura leucomelana*) R
140. Silver Pheasant (*Lophura nycthemera*) R
141. Crested Fireback (*Lophura ignita*) R
142. Siamese Fireback (*Lophura diardi*) R *
143. Red Junglefowl (*Gallus gallus*) R *
144. Hume's Pheasant (*Syrmaticus humiae*) R
145. Grey Peacock-Pheasant (*Polypectron bicalcaratum*) R
146. Malaysian Peacock Pheasant (*Polypectron malacense*) R?
147. Great Argus (*Argusianus argus*) R
148. Green Peafowl (*Pavo muticus*) R

Turnicidae : BUTTONQUAIL
149. Little Buttonquail (*Turnix sylvatica*) R
150. Yellow-legged Buttonquail (*Turnix tanki*) R

151. Barred Buttonquail (*Turnix suscitator*) R

Gruidae : CRANES
152. Sarus Crane (*Grus antigone*) E

Rallidae : RAILS, CRAKES, COOTS
153. Water Rail (*Rallus aquaticus*) V
154 Slaty-breasted Rail (*Rallus striatus*) R
155. Red-legged Crake (*Rallina fasciata*) R & V
156. Slaty-legged Crake (*Rallina eurizonoides*) R? & V
157. Baillon's Crake (*Porzana pusilla*) V
158. Spotted Crake (*Porzana porzana*) A
159. Ruddy-breasted Crake (*Porzana fusca*) R & V
160. Band-bellied Crake (*Porzana paykullii*) A
161. Black-tailed Crake (*Porzana bicolor*) R
162. White-browed Crake (*Porzana cinerea*) R *
163. White-breasted Waterhen (*Amaurornis phoenicurus*) R *
164. Watercock (*Gallicrex cinerea*) R & N
165. Common Moorhen (*Gallinula chloropus*) R & V
166. Purple Swamphen ((*Porphyrio porphyrio*) R *
167. Common Coot (*Fulica atra*) V

Heliornithidae : FINFOOTS
168. Masked Finfoot (*Heliopais personata*) V & R?

Jacanidae : JACANAS
169. Pheasant-tailed Jacana (*Hydrophasianus chirurgus*) R & V
170. Bronzed-winged Jacana (*Metopidius indicus*) R

Rostratulidae : PAINTEDSNIPE
171. Greater Paintedsnipe (*Rostratula benghalensis*) R

Charadriidae : LAPWINGS, PLOVERS
172. Northern Lapwing (*Vanellus vanellus*) V
173. Grey-headed Lapwing (*Vanellus cinereus*) V
174. Red-wattled Lapwing (*Vanellus indicus*) R *
175. River Lapwing (*Vanellus duvaucellii*) R
176. Grey Plover (*Pluvialis squatarola*) V
177. Pacific Golden Plover (*Pluvialis fulva*) V
178. Little Ringed Plover (*Charadrius dubius*) R & V *
179. Kentish Plover (*Charadrius alexandrinus*) V
180. Malaysian Plover (*Charadrius peronii*) R
181. Long-billed Plover (*Charadrius placidus*) V
182. Mongolian Plover (*Charadrius mongolus*) V

183. Greater Sand-Plover (*Charadrius leschenaultii*) V

Scolopacidae : CURLEWS, GODWITS, SANDPIPERS, SNIPE
184. Eurasian Curlew (*Numenius arquata*) V
185. Whimbrel (*Numenius phaeopus*) V
186. Eastern Curlew (*Numenius madagascariensis*) V
187. Little Curlew *(Numenius minutus)* A
188. Black-tailed Godwit (*Limosa limosa*) V
189. Bar-tailed Godwit (*Limosa lapponica*) V
190. Spotted Redshank (*Tringa erythropus*) V
191. Common Redshank (*Tringa totanus*) V *
192. Marsh Sandpiper (*Tringa stagnatilis*) V *
193. Common Greenshank (*Tringa nebularia*) V *
194. Nordman's Greenshank (*Tringa guttifer*) V
195. Green Sandpiper (*Tringa ocrophus*) V
196. Wood Sandpiper (*Tringa glareola*) V
197. Terek Sandpiper (*Xenus cinereus*) V
198. Common Sandpiper (*Actitis hypoleucos*) V *
199. Grey-tailed Tattler (*Heteroscelus brevipes*) V
200. Ruddy Turnstone (*Arenaria interpres*) V
201. Asian Dowitcher (*Limnodromus semipalmatus*) V
202. Long-billed Dowitcher (*Limnodromus scolopaceus*) A
203. Wood Snipe (*Gallinago nemoricola*) A
204. Pintail Snipe (*Gallinago stenura*) V
205. Swinhoe's Snipe (*Gallinago megala*) A
206. Common Snipe (*Gallinago gallinago*) V
207. Jack Snipe (*Lymnocryptes minimus*) V
208. Eurasian Woodcock (*Scolopax rusticola*) V209.
209. Red Knot (*Calidris canutus*) V
210. Great Knot (*Calidris tenuirostris*) V
211. Rufous-necked Stint (*Calidris ruficollis*) V *
212. Long-toed Stint (*Calidris subminuta*) V
213. Temminck's Stint (*Calidris temminckii*) V *
214. Little Stint (*Calidris minuta*) A
215. Curlew Sandpiper (*Calidris ferruginea*) V
216. Sanderling (*Calidris alba*) V
217. Dunlin (*Calidris alpina*) V
218. Sharp-tailed Sandpiper (*Calidris acuminata*) A
219. Spoon-billed Sandpiper (*Eurynorhynchus pygmaeus*) V
220. Broad-billed Sandpiper (*Limicola falcinellus*) V
221. Ruff (*Philomachus pugnax*) V

Phalaropopidae : PHALAROPES

222. Red-necked Phalarope (*Phalaropus lobatus*) V

Recurvirostridae : STILTS, AVOCETS
223. Black-winged Stilt (*Himantopus himantopus*) R & V
224. Pied Avocet (*Recurvirostra avosetta*) A

Dromadidae : CRAB PLOVER
225. Crab Plover (*Dromas ardeola*) V

Burhinidae : THICK-KNEES
226. Stone Curlew (*Burhinus oedicnemus*) R? & V
227. Beach Thick-Knee (*Esacus magnirostris*) R
228. Great Thick-Knee (*Esacus recurvirostris*) E?

Glareolidae : PRATINCOLES
229. Oriental Pratincole (*Glareola maldivarum*) N
230. Small Pratincole (*Glareola lactea)* R & V

Stercoraiidae : JAEGERS, SKUAS
231. Pomarine Jaeger (*Stercorarius pomarinus*) V
232. Parasitic Jaeger (*Stercorarius parasiticus*) V & A
233. Long-tailed Jaeger (*Stercorarius longicaudus*) A .

Laridae: Gulls, Terns
234. Great Black-headed Gull (*Larus ictihyaetus*) A
235. Common Black-headed Gull (*Larus ridibundus*) V *
236. Brown-headed Gull (*Larus brunnicephalus*) V *
237. Herring Gull (*Larus argentatus*) V
238. Slender-billed Gull (*Larus genei*) V
239. Black-tailed Gull (*Larus crassirostris*) A
240. Whiskered Tern (*Chlidonias hybridus*) V *
241. White-winged Tern (*Chlidonias leucopterus*) V *
242. Gull-billed Tern (*Gelochelidon nilotica*) V
243. Caspian Tern (*Sterna caspia*) V
244. River Tern (*Sterna aurantia*) R? A
245. Common Tern (*Sterna hirundo*) V
246. Roseate Tern (*Sterna dougallii*) R
247. Black-naped Tern (*Sterna sumatrana*) R
248. Black-bellied Tern (*Sterna acuticauda*) R?
249. Bridled Tern (*Sterna anaethetus*) R
250. Sooty Tern (*Sterna fuscata*) A
251. Little Tern (*Sterna albifrons*) R
252. Saunder's Tern (*Sterna saundersi*) A
253. Great Crested Tern (*Sterna bergii*) R & V *
254. Lesser Crested Tern (*Sterna bengalensis*) V *

255. Chinese Crested-Tern (*Sterna bernsteinii*) A & E

256. Brown Noddy (*Anous stolidus*) R? & V

Rhynchopidae : SKIMMERS

257. Indian Skimmer (*Rynchops albicollis*) A

Columbidae : PIGEONS, DOVES

258. Pin-tailed Pigeon (*Treron apicauda*) R & V

259. Yellow-vented Pigeon (*Treron seimundi*) R?

260. Wedge-tailed Pigeon (*Treron sphenura*) R

261. White-bellied Pigeon (*Treron seiboldii*) R?

262. Thick-billed Pigeon (*Treron curvirostra*) R *

263. Pompadour.Pigeon (*Treron pompadora*) R *

264. Cinnamon-headed Pigeon (*Treron fulvicollis*) R?

265. Little Green Pigeon (*Treron olax*) R

266. Pink-necked Pigeon (*Treron vernans*) R *

267. Orange-breasted Pigeon (*Treron bicincta*) R

268. Large Green Pigeon (*Treron capellei*) R

269. Yellow-footed Pigeon (*Treron phoenicoptera*) R

270. Jambu Fruit-Dove (*Ptilinopus jambu*) R

271. Green Imperial Pigeon (*Ducula aenea*) R *

272. Mountain Imperial Pigeon (*Ducula badia*) R *

273. Pied Imperial Pigeon (*Ducula bicolor*) R

274. Rock Pigeon (*Columba livia*) R

275. Speckled Wood-Pigeon (*Columba hodgsonii*) V

276. Ashy Wood-Pigeon (*Columba pulchricollis*) R

277. Pale-capped Pigeon (*Columba punicea*) R? & V

278. Barred Cuckoo-Dove (*Macropygia unchall*) R

279. Little Cuckoo-Dove (*Macropygia ruficeps*) R

280. Spotted Dove (*Streptopelia chinensis*) R*

281. Oriental Turtle Dove (*Streptopelia orientalis*) R & V *

282. Red Turtle Dove (*Streptopelia tranquebarica*) R *

283. Peaceful Dove (*Geopelia striata*) R

284. Green-winged Pigeon (*Chalcophaps indica*) R *

285. Nicobar Pigeon (*Caloenas nicobarica)* R

Psittacidae : PARROTS

286. Alexandrine Parakeet (*Psittacula eupatria*) R

287. Red-breasted Parakeet (*Psittacula alexandri*) R *

288. Blossom-headed Parakeet (*Psittacula roseata*) R *

289. Grey-headed Parakeet (*Psittacula finschii*) R *

290. Blue-rumped Parrot (*Psittinus cyanurus*) R

291. Vernal Hanging Parrot (*Loriculus vernalis*) R *

292. Blue-crowned Hanging Parrot (*Loriculus galgulus*) R *

Cuculidae : CUCKOOS

293. Chestnut-winged Cuckoo (*Clamator coromandus*) N & V

294. Large Hawk-Cuckoo (*Cuculus sparverioides*) R & V

295. Common Hawk-Cuckoo (*Cuculus varius*) A

296. Moustached Hawk-Cuckoo (*Cuculus vagans)* R

297. Hodgson's Hawk-Cuckoo (*Cuculus fugax*) R & V

298. Indian Cuckoo (*Cuculus micropterus*) R & V

299. Common Cuckoo (*Cuculus canorus*) R?

300. Oriental Cuckoo (*Cuculus saturatus*) V

301. Lesser Cuckoo (*Cuculus poliocephalus*) A

302. Banded Bay Cuckoo (*Cacomantis sonneratii*) R *

303. Plaintive Cuckoo (*Cacomantis merulinus*) R *

304. Brush Cuckoo (*Cacomantis sepulcralis*) R

305. Asian Emerald Cuckoo (*Chrysococcyx maculatus*) R & V

306. Violet Cuckoo (*Chrysococcyx xanthorhynchus*) R & V

307. Malayan Bronze Cuckoo (*Chrysoccoccyx minutillus*)

308. Drongo Cuckoo (*Surniculus lugubris*) R & V

309. Common Koel (*Eudynamys scolopacea*) R *

310. Black-bellied Malkoha (*Phaenicophaeus diardi*) R *

311. Chestnut-bellied Malkoha (*Phaenicophaeus sumatranus*) R

312. Green-billed Malkoha (*Phaenicophaeus tristis*) R *

313. Raffle's Malkoha (*Phaenicophaeus chlorophaeus*) R

314. Red-billed Malkoha (*Phaenicophaeus javanicus*) R

315. Chestnut-breasted Malkoha (*Phaenicophaeus curvirostris*) R

316. Coral-billed Ground-Cuckoo (*Carpococcyx renauldi*) R

317. Greater Coucal (*Centropus sinensis*) R *

318. Lesser Coucal (*Centropus bengalensis*) R *.

Strigidae : OWLS
319. Barn Owl (*Tyto alba*) R
320. Bay Owl (*Phodilus badius*) R
321. White-fronted Scops-Owl (*Otus sagittatus*) R
322. Reddish Scops-Owl (*Otus rufescens*) R
323. Mountain Scops-Owl (*Otus spilocephalus*) R
324. Common Scops-Owl (*Otus sunia*) R & V
325. Collared Scops-Owl (*Otus lempiji*) R *
326. Spot-bellied Eagle Owl (*Bubo nipalensis*) R
327. Barred Eagle-Owl (Bubo *sumatranus*) R
328. Dusky Eagle-Owl (*Bubo coromandus*) R?
329. Brown Fish-Owl (*Ketupa zeylonensis*) R
330. Buffy Fish-Owl (*Ketupa ketupu*) R
331. Collared Owlet (*Glaucidium brodiei*) R
332. Asian Barred-Owl (*Glaucidium cuculoides*) R *
333. Brown Hawk-Owl (*Ninox scutulata*) R & V
334. Spotted Owlet (*Athene brama*) R *
335. Spotted Wood-Owl (*Strix seloputo*) R
336. Brown Wood-Owl (*Strix leptogrammica*) R
337. Short-eared Owl (*Asio flammeus*) A.

Podargidae : FROGMOUTHS
338. Large Frogmouth (*Batrachostomus auritus*) R
339. Gould's Frogmouth (*Brtrachostomus stellatus*) R
340. Hodgson's Frogmouth (*Batrachostomus hodgsoni)* R
341. Javan Frogmouth (*Batrachostomus javensis)* R

Caprimulgidae : NIGHTJARS
342. Great-eared Nightjar (*Eurostopodus macrotis)* R
343. Malaysian-eared Nightjar (*Eurostopodus temminckii*) R
344. Grey Nightjar (*Caprimulgus indicus*) R & V
345. Large-tailed Nightjar (*Caprimulgus macrurus*) R *
346. Indian Nightjar (*Caprimulgus asiaticus*) R *
347. Savanna Nightjar (*Caprimulgus affinis*) R

Apodidae : SWIFTS
348. Edible-nest Swiftlet (*Aerodramus fuciphagus*) R *
349. Black-nest Swiftlet (*Aerodramus maximus*) R *
350. Himalayan Swiftlet (*Aerodramus brevirostris*) R & V
351. White-bellied Swiftlet (*Collocalia esculenta*) R

352. White-throated Needletail (*Hirundapus caudacutus)* V
353. White-vented Needletail (*Hirundapus cochinchinensis*) V
354. Brown Needletail (*Hirundapus giganteus)* R
355. Silver-rumped Swift (*Rhaphidura leucopygialis*) R
356. Dark-rumped Swift (*Apus acuticauda*) R
357. Fork-tailed Swift (*Apus pacificus*) R & V
358. House Swift (*Apus affinis*) R
359. Asian Palm Swift (*Cypsiurus balasiensis*) R *

Hemiprocnidae : TREESWIFTS
360. Crested Treeswift (*Hemiprocne coronota*) R
361. Grey-rumped Treeswift (*Hemiprocne longipennis*) R
362. Whiskered Treeswift (*Hemiprocne comata*) R

Trogonidae : TROGONS
363. Red-naped Trogon (*Harpactes kasumba*) R
364. Diard's Trogon (*Harpactes diardii*) R
365. Cinnamon-rumped Trogon (*Harpactes orrhophaeus*) R
366. Scarlet-rumped Trogon (*Harpactes duvaucelii*) R
367. Orange-breasted Trogon (*Harpactes oreskios*) R *
368. Red-headed Trogon (*Harpactes erythrocephalus*) R

Alcedinidae : KINGFISHERS
369. Crested Kingfisher (*Megaceryle lugubris*) R
370. Pied Kingfisher (*Ceryle rudis*) R
371. Blyth's Kingfisher (*Alcedo hercules*) A
372. Common Kingfisher (*Alcedo atthis*) V & R *
373. Blue-eared Kingfisher (*Alcedo meninting*) R *
374. Blue-banded Kingfisher (*Alcedo euryzona*) R
375. Black-backed Kingfisher (*Ceyx erithacus*) R & V
376. Banded Kingfisher (*Lacedo pulchella*) R
377. Brown-winged Kingfisher (*Pelargopsis amauroptera*) R
378. Stork-billed Kingfisher (*Halcyon capensis*) R
379. Ruddy Kingfisher (*Halcyon coromanda*) R & V
380. White-throated Kingfisher (*Halcyon smyrnensis*) R *
381. Black-capped Kingfisher (*Halcyon pileata*) V *

382. Collared Kingfisher (*Halcyon chloris*) R *
383. Rufous-collared Kingfisher (*Actenoides concretus*) R

Meropidae : **BEE-EATERS**
384. Chestnut-headed Bee-eater (*Merops leschenaulti*) R *
385. Blue-tailed Bee-eater (*Merops philippinus*) R & V
386. Green Bee-eater (*Merops orientalis*) R *
387. Blue-throated Bee-eater (*Merops viridis*) R & V
388. Red-bearded Bee-eater (*Nyctyornis amictus*) R
389. Blue-bearded Bee-eater *(Nyctyornis athertoni)* R

Coraciidae : **ROLLERS**
390. Indian Roller (*Coracias benghalensis*) R *
391. Dollarbird (*Eurystomus orientalis*) R & V *

Upupidae : **HOOPOE**
392. Hoopoe (*Upupa epops*) R

Bucerotidae : **HORNBILLS**
393. White-crowned Hornbill (*Berenicornis comatus*) R
394. Brown Hornbill (*Ptilolaemus tickelli*) R
395. Bushy-crested Hornbill (*Anorrhinus galeritus*) R
396. Rufous-necked Hornbill (*Aceros nipalensis*) R
397. Wrinkled Hornbill (*Rhyticeros corrugatus*) R?
398. Wreathed Hornbill (*Rhyticeros undulatus*) R
399. Blyth's Hornbill (*Rhyticeros subruficollis*) R
400. Black Hornbill (*Anthracoceros malayanus*) R
401. Indian Pied Hornbill (*Anthracoceros albirostris*) R *
402. Rhinoceros Hornbill (*Buceros rhinoceros*) R *
403. Great Hornbill (*Buceros bicornis*) R *
404. Helmeted Hornbill (*Rhinoplax vigil*) R

Capitonidae : **BARBETS**
405. Great Barbet (*Megalaima virens*) R
406. Lineated Barbet (*Megalaima lineata*) R *
407. Green-eared Barbet (*Megalaima faiostricta*) R
408. Gold-whiskered Barbet (*Megalaima chrysopogon*) R
409. Red-crowned Barbet (*Megalaima rafflesii*) R
410. Red-throated Barbet (*Megalaima mystacophanos*) R

411. Golden-throated Barbet (*Megalaima franklinii*) R
412. Blue-throated Barbet (*Megalaima asiatica*) R *
413. Moustached Barbet (*Megalaima incognita*) R
414. Yellow-crowned Barbet (*Megalaima henricii)* R
415. Blue-eared Barbet (*Megalaima australis*) R *
416. Coppersmith Barbet (*Megalaima haemacephala*) R *
417. Brown Barbet (*Calorhamphus fuliginosus*) R

Indicatoridae : **HONEYGUIDES**
418. Malaysian Honeyguide (*Indicator archipelagicus*) R

Picidae : **WOODPECKERS**
419. Eurasian Wryneck (*Jynx torquilla*) V
420. Speckled Piculet (*Picumnus innominatus*) R
421. White-browed Piculet (*Sasia ochracea*) R
422. Rufous Piculet (*Sasia abnormis*) R
423. Rufous Woodpecker (*Celeus brachyurus*) R
424. Laced Woodpecker (*Picus vittatus*) R *
425. Streak-breasted Woodpecker (*Picus viridanus*) R *
426. Streak-throated Woodpecker (*Picus xanthopygaeus*) R *
427. Grey-headed Woodpecker (*Picus canus*) R
428. Black-headed Woodpecker (*Picus erythropygius)* R
429. Greater Yellownape (*Picus flavinucha*) R *
430. Crimson-winged Woodpecker (*Picus puniceus*) R
431. Lesser Yellownape (*Picus chlorolophus*) R
432. Checker-throated Woodpecker (*Picus mentalis*) R
433. Banded Woodpecker (*Picus miniaceus*) R
434. Common Goldenback (*Dinopium javanense*) R
435. Olive-backed Woodpecker (*Dinopium rafflesii*) R
436. Pale-headed Woodpecker (*Gecinulus grantia*) R?
437. Bamboo Woodpecker (*Gecinulus tristis*) R
439. Black-and-Buff Woodpecker (*Meiglyptes jugularis*) R
440. Buff-necked Woodpecker (*Meiglyptes tukki*) R
441. Great Slaty Woodpecker (*Mulleripicus pulverulentus*) R
442. White-bellied Woodpecker (*Dryocopus javensis*) R
443. Crimson-breasted Woodpecker (*Picoides cathpharius*) R

444. Rufous-bellied Woodpecker (*Picoides hyperythrus*) R
445. Stripe-breasted Woodpecker (*Picoides atratus*) R
446. Fulvous-breasted Woodpecker (*Picoides macei*) R
447. Yellow-crowned Woodpecker (*Picoides mahrattensis*) R
448. Grey-capped Woodpecker (*Picoides canicapillus*) R *
449. Grey-and-Buff Woodpecker (*Hemicircus concretus*) R
450. Heart-spotted Woodpecker ((*Hemicircus canente*) R
451. Bay Woodpecker (*Blythipicus pyrrhotis*) R
452. Maroon Woodpecker (*Blythipicus rubiginosus*) R
453. Greater Goldenback (*Chrysocolaptes lucidus*) R *
454. Orange-backed Woodpecker (*Reinwardtipicus validus*) R

Eurylaimidae : BROADBILLS
455. Dusky Broadbill (*Corydon sumatranus*) R
456. Black-and-Red Broadbill (*Cymbirhynchus macrorhynchus*) R *
457. Banded Broadbill (*Eurylaimus javanicus*) R
458. Black-and-Yellow Broadbill (*Eurylaimus ochromalus*) R
459. Silver-breasted Broadbill (*Serilophus lunatus*) R
460. Long-tailed Broadbill (*Psarisomus dalhousiae*) R
461. Green Broadbill (*Calyptomena viridis*) R

Pittidae : PITTAS
462. Rusty-naped Pitta *(Pitta oatesi)* R
463. Blue-rumped Pitta (*Pitta soror*) R
464. Giant Pitta (*Pitta caerulea*) R
465. Blue-winged Pitta (*Pitta moluccensis*) N & V *
466. Garnet Pitta (*Pitta granatina*) R
467. Mangrove Pitta (*Pitta megarhyncha*) R *
468. Hooded Pitta (*Pitta sordida*) N
469. Bar-bellied Pitta (*Pitta ellioti*) R
470. Blue Pitta (*Pitta cyanea*) R
471. Banded Pitta (*Pitta guajana*) R
472. Gurney's Pitta (*Pitta gurneyi*) R
473. Eared Pitta (*Pitta phayrei}* R

Alaudidae : LARKS
474. Singing Bushlark (*Mirafra javanica*) R
475. Rufous-winged Bushlark (*Mirafra assamica*) R
476. Oriental Skylark (*Alauda gulgula*) R & V?

Hirundinidae : SWALLOWS
477. White-eyed River-Martin (*Pseudochelidon sirintarae*) E?
478. Plain Martin (*Riparia paludicola*) V
479. Sand Martin (*Riparia riparia*) V
480. Dusky Crag Martin (*Hirundo concolor*) R
481. Barn Swallow (*Hirundo rustica*) V & R? *
482. Pacific Swallow (*Hirundo tahitica*) R *
483. Wire-tailed Swallow (*Hirundo smithii*) R
484. Red-rumped Swallow (*Hirundo daurica)* R & V
485. Common House-Martin (*Delichon urbica*) V
486. Asian House-Martin (*Delichon dasypus*) V
487. Nepal House-Martin (*Delichon nipalensis*)

Campephagidae : CUCKOO-SHRIKES, MINIVETS
488. Bar-winged Flycatcher Shrike *(Hemipus picatus)* R
489. Black-winged Flycatcher Shrike (*Hemipus hirundinaceus*) R
490. Large Wood-Shrike (*Tephrodornis virgatus*) R *
491. Common Wood-Shrike (*Tephrodornis pondicerianus*) R *
492. Large Cuckoo-Shrike (*Coracina macei*) R
493. Bar-bellied Cuckoo-Shrike (*Coracina striata*) R
494. Indochinese Cuckoo-Shrike (*Coracina polioptera*) R
495. Black-winged Cuckoo-Shrike (*Coracina melachista*) R & V
496. Lesser Cuckoo-Shrike (*Coracina fimbriata*) R
497. Pied Triller (*Lalage nigra*) R
498. Ashy Minivet (*Pericrocotus divaricatus*) V
499. Rosy Minivet (*Pericrocotus roseus*) R
500. Small Minivet (*Pericrocotus cinnamomeus*) R
501. Fiery Minivet (*Pericrocotus igneus*) R
502. Grey-chinned Minivet (*Pericrocotus solaris*) R
503. Short-billed Minivet (*Pericrocotus brevirostris*) R
504. Long-tailed Minivet (*Pericrocotus ethologus*) R & V
505. Scarlet Minivet (*Pericrocotus flammeus*) R *

Chloropseidae : IORAS, LEAFBIRDS
506. Green Iora (*Aegithina viridissima*) R
507. Common Iora (*Aegithina tiphia*) R *
508. Great Iora (*Aegithina lafresnayei*) R *
509. Lesser Green Leafbird (*Chloropsis cyanopogon*) R

510. Greater Green Leafbird (*Chloropsis sonnerati*) R
511. Golden-fronted Leafbird (*Chloropsis aurifrons*) R
512. Blue-winged Leafbird (*Chloropsis cochinchinensis*) R
513. Orange-bellied Leafbird (*Chloropsis hardwickii*) R

Pycnonotidae : BULBULS
514. Crested Finchbill (*Spizixos canifrons*) R
515. Straw-headed Bulbul (*Pycnonotus zeylanicus*) R
516. Black-and-White Bulbul (*Pycnonotus melanoleucos*) R
517. Striated Bulbul (*Pycnonotus striatus*) R
518. Black-headed Bulbul (*Pycnonotus atriceps*) R *
519. Black-crested Bulbul (*Pycnonotus melanicterus*) R *
520. Scaly-breasted Bulbul (*Pycnonotus squamatus*) R
521. Grey-bellied Bulbul (*Pycnonotus cyaniventris*) R
522. Red-whiskered Bulbul (*Pycnonotus jocosus*) R *
523. Brown-bellied Bulbul (*Pycnonotus xanthorrhous*) R
524. Sooty-headed Bulbul (*Pycnonotus aurigaster*) R *
525. Puff-backed Bulbul (*Pycnonotus eutilotus*) R
526. Stripe-throated Bulbul (*Pycnonotus finlaysoni*) R
527. Flavescent Bulbul (*Pycnonotus flavescens*) R
528. Yellow-vented Bulbul (*Pycnonotus goiavier*) R *
529. Olive-winged Bulbul (*Pycnonotus plumosus*) R *
530. Streak-eared Bulbul (*Pycnonotus blanfordi*) R *
531. Cream-vented Bulbul (*Pycnonotus simplex*) R
532. Red-eyed Bulbul (*Pycnonotus brunneus*) R
534. Spectacled Bulbul (*Pycnonotus erythropthalmos*) R
535. Light-vented Bulbul (*Pycnonotus sinensis*) V?
536. Finsch's Bulbul (*Criniger finschii*) R
537. White-throated Bulbul (*Criniger flaveolus*) R
538. Puff-throated Bulbul (*Criniger pallidus*) R
539. Ochraceous Bulbul (*Criniger ochraeus*) R
540. Grey-cheeked Bulbul (*Criniger bres*) R
541. Yellow-bellied Bulbul (*Criniger phaeocephalus*) R
542. Hairy-backed Bulbul (*Hypsipetes criniger*) R
543. Olive Bulbul (*Hypsipetes viridescens*) R
544. Grey-eyed Bulbul (*Hypsipetes propinquus*) R
545. Buff-vented Bulbul (*Hypsipetes charlottae*) R
546. Mountain Bulbul (*Hypsipetes mcclellandii*) R
547. Streaked Bulbul (*Hypsipetes malaccensis*) R
548. Chestnut Bulbul (*Hypsipetes flavala*) R
549. Black Bulbul (*Hypsipetes madagascariensis*) R & V
550. White-headed Bulbul (*Hypsipetes thompsoni*) R & V?

Dicruridae : DRONGOS
551. Black Drongo (*Dicrurus macrocercus*) R & V *
552. Ashy Drongo (*Dicrurus leucophaeus*) R & V *
553. Crow-billed Drongo (*Dicrurus annectans*) V & N?
554. Bronzed Drongo (*Dicrurus aeneus*) R
555. Lesser Racket-tailed Drongo (*Dicrurus remifer*) R *
556. Spangled Drongo (*Dicrurus hottentottus*) R & V
557. Greater Racker-tailed Drongo (*Dicrurus paradiseus*) R *

Oriolidae : ORIOLES
558. Dark-throated Oriole (*Oriolus xanthonotus*) R
559. Black-naped Oriole (*Oriolus chinensis*) V & R? *
560. Slender-billed Oriole (*Oriolus tenuirostris*) V & R? *
561. Black-hooded Oriole (*Oriolus xanthornus*) R *
562. Maroon Oriole (*Oriolus traillii*) R & V
563. Silver Oriole (*Oriolus mellianus*) V

Irenidae : FAIRY-BLUEBIRDS
564. Asian Fairy-Bluebird (*Irena puella*) R *

Corvidae : JAYS, MAGPIES, CROWS
565. Crested Jay (*Platylophus galericulatus*) R
566. Eurasian Jay (*Garrulus glandarius*) R
567. Short-tailed Magpie (*Cissa hypoleuca*) R
568. Green Magpie (*Cissa chinensis*) R
569. Blue Magpie (*Cissa erythrorhyncha*) R *
570. Black-billed Magpie (*Pica pica*) A
571. Rufous Treepie (*Dendrocitta vagabunda*) R
572. Grey Treepie (*Dendrocitta formosae*) R

573. Racket-tailed Treepie (*Crypsirina temia*) R
574. Black Magpie (*Platysmurus leucopterus*) R
575. Large-billed Crow (*Corvus macrorhynchos*) R *
576. House Crow (*Corvus splendens*) E?

Aegithalidae : **LONG-TAILED TITS**
577. Black-throated Tit (*Aegithalos concinnus*) R

Remizidae : **PENDULINE TITS**
578. Fire-capped Tit (*Cephalopyrus flammiceps*) A

Paridae : **TYPICAL TITS**
579. Great Tit (*Parus major*) R
580. Yellow-cheeked Tit (*Parus spilonotus*) R
581. Sultan Tit (*Melanochlora sultanea*) R
582. Yellow-browed Tit (*Sylviparus modestus*) R

Sittidae : **NUTHATCHES**
583. Chestnut-bellied Nuthatch (*Sitta castanea*) R
584. Chestnut-vented Nuthatch (*Sitta nagaensis*) R
585. Velvet-fronted Nuthatch (*Sitta frontalis*) R *
586. Giant Nuthatch (*Sitta magna*) R
587. Beautiful Nuthatch (*Sitta formosa*) R

Certhiidae : **NORTHERN TREECREEPER**
588. Brown-throated Treecreeper (*Certhia discolor*) R

Cinclidae : **DIPPERS**
589. Brown Dipper (*Cinclus pallasii*) R

Timaliidae : **BABBLERS**
590. Puff-throated Babbler (*Pellorneum ruficeps*) R *
591. Black-capped Babbler (*Pellorneum capistratum*) R
592. Spot-throated Babbler (*Pellorneum albiventre*) R
593 Buff-breasted Babbler (*Trichastoma tickelli*) R
594. Short-tailed Babbler (*Trichastoma malaccense*) R
595. White-chested Babbler (*Trichastoma rostratum*) R
596. Ferruginous Babbler (*Trichastoma) bicolor*) R
597. Horsfield's Babbler (*Trichastoma sepiarium*) R
598. Abbott's Babbler (*Trichastoma abbotti*) R
699. Moustached Babbler (*Malacopteron magnirostre*) R

600. Sooty-capped Babbler (*Malacopteron affine*) R
601. Scaly-crowned Babbler *(Malacopteron cinereum*) R
602. Rufous-crowned Babbler (*Malacopteron magnum*) R
603. Large Scimitar-Babbler (*Pomatorhinus hypoleucos*) R
604. Rusty-cheeked Scimitar-Babbler (*Pomatorhinus erythrogenys*) R
605. White-browed Scimitar-Babbler (*Pomatorhinus schisticeps*) R *
606. Red-billed Scimitar-Babbler (*Pomatorhinus ochraceiceps*) R
607. Coral-billed Scimitar-Babbler (*Pomatorhinus ferruginosus*) R
608. Striped Wren-Babbler (*Kenopia striata*) R
609. Large Wren-Babbler (*Napothera macrodactyla*) R
610. Limestone Wren-Babbler (*Napothera crispifrons*) R
611. Streaked Wren-Babbler (*Napothera brevicaudata*) R
612. Eye-browed Wren-Babbler (*Napothera epilepidota*) R
613. Pygmy Wren-Babbler (*Pnoepyga pusilla*) R
614. Deignan's Babbler (*Stachyris rodolphei*) R
615. Rufous-fronted Babbler (*Stachyris rufifrons*) R
616. Golden Babbler (*Stachyris chrysaea*) R
617. Grey-throated Babbler (*Stachyris nigriceps*) R
618. Grey-headed Babbler (*Stachyris poliocephala*) R
619. Spot-necked Babbler (*Stachyris striolata*) R
620. Chestnut-rumped Babbler (*Stachyris maculata*) R
621. White-necked Babbler (*Stachyris leucotis*) R
622. Black-throated Babbler (*Stachyris nigricollis*) R
623. Chestnut-winged Babbler (*Stachyris erythroptera*) R
624. Striped Tit-Babbler (*Macronous gularis*) R *
625. Fluffy-backed Tit-Babbler (*Macronous ptilosus*) R
626. Chestnut-capped Babbler (*Timalia pileata*) R
627. Yellow-eyed Babbler (*Chrysomma sinense*) R
628. White-crested Laughingthrush (*Garrulax leucolophus*) R *
629. Lesser Necklaced Laughingthrush (*Garrulax monileger*)
630. Greater Necklaced Laughingthrush (*Garrulax pectoralis*) R *

631. White-necked Laughingthrush (*Garrulax strepitans*) R
632. White-browed Laughingthrush (*Garrulax sannio*) R
633. Black-throated Laughingthrush (*Garrulax chinensis*) R
634. Spot-breasted Laughingthrush (*Garrulax merulinus*) R
635. Chestnut-crowned Laughingthrush (*Garrulax erythrocephalus*) R
636. Red-tailed Laughingthrush (*Garrulax milnei*) R
637. Red-faced Liocichla (*Liocichla phoenicea*) R
638. Silver-eared Mesia (*Leiothrix argentauris*) R
639. Cutia (*Cutia nipalensis*) R
640. White-browed Shrike-Babbler (*Pteruthius flaviscapis*) R
641. Black-eared Shrike-Babbler (*Pteruthius melanotis*) R
642. Chestnut-fronted Shrike-Babbler (*Pteruthius aenobarbus*) R
643. White-hooded Babbler (*Gampsorhynchus rufulus*) R
644. Spectacled Barwing (*Actinodura ramsayi*) R
645. Blue-winged Minla (*Minla cyanouroptera*) R
646. Chestnut-tailed Minla (*Minla strigula*) R
647. Rufous-winged Fulvetta (*Alcippe castaneceps*) R
648. Rufous-throated Fulvetta (*Alcippe rufogularis*) R
649. Brown Fulvetta (*Alcippe brunneicauda*) R
650. Brown-cheeked Fulvetta (*Alcippe poioicephala*) R
651. Mountain Fulvetta (*Alcippe peracensis*) R
652. Grey-cheeked Fulvetta (*Alcippe morrisonia*) R
653. Rufous-backed Sibia (*Heterophasia annectens*) R
654. Black-headed Sibia (*Heterophasia melanoleuca*) R
655. Long-tailed Sibia (*Heterophasia picaoides*) R
656. Striated Yuhina (*Yuhina castaniceps*) R
657. Whiskered Yuhina (*Yuhina flavicollis*) R
658. Burmese Yuhina (*Yuhina humilis*) R
659. White-bellied Yuhina (*Yuhina zantholeuca*) R *
660. Malaysian Rail-Babbler (*Eupetes macrocerus*) R

Paradoxornithidae : PARROTBILLS
661. Short-tailed Parrotbill (*Paradoxornis davidianus*)

662. Spot-breasted Parrotbill (*Paradoxornis guttaticollis*) R
663. Black-throated Parrotbill (*Paradoxornis nipalensis*) R
664. Short-tailed Parrotbill (*Parodoxornis atrosuperciliaris*) R
665. Grey-headed Parrotbill (*Paradoxornis gularis*) R

Turdidae : THRUSHES
666. Lesser Shortwing (*Brachypteryx leucophrys*) R
667. White-browed Shortwing (*Brachypteryx montana*) R
668. Japanese Robin (*Erithacus akahige*) R
669. Rufous-tailed Robin (*Luscinia sibilans*) V
670. Siberian Rubythroat (*Luscinia calliope*) V
671. White-tailed Rubythroat (*Luscinia pectoralis*) A
672. Bluethroat (*Luscinia svecicus*) V
673. Black-throated Robin (*Luscinia obscurus*) A
674. Siberian Blue Robin (*Luscinia cyane*) V
675 Orange-flanked Bush-Robin (*Tarsiger cyanurus*) V
676. Golden Bush-Robin (*Tarsiger chrysaeus*) V
677. Magpie Robin (*Copsychus saularis*) R *
678. White-rumped Shama (*Copsychus malabaricus*) R *
679. Rufous-tailed Shama (*Copsychus pyrropygus*) R
680. Blue-fronted Redstart (*Phoenicurus frontalis*) V
681. Daurian Redstart (*Phoenicurus auroreus*) V
682. Plumbeous Redstart (*Rhyacornis fuliginosus*) R & V?
683. White-bellied Redstart (*Hodgsonius phaenicuroides*) V
684. River Chat (*Chaimarrornis leucocephalus*) V
685. White-tailed Robin (*Cinclidium leucurum*) R
686. Blue-fronted Robin (*Cinclidium frontale*) A
687. Chestnut-naped Forktail (*Enicurus ruficapillus*) R
688. Black-backed Forktail (*Enicurus immaculatus*) R
689. Slaty-backed Forktail (*Enicurus schistaceus*) R
690. White-crowned Forktail (*Enicurus leschenaulti*) R
691. Purple cochoa (*Cochoa purpurea*) R
692. Green Cochoa (*Cochoa viridis*) R
693. Stonechat (*Saxicola torquata*) V & R
694. Pied Bushchat (*Saxicola caprata*) R *
695. Jerdon's Bushchat (*Saxicola jerdoni*) R
696. Grey Bushchat (*Saxicola ferrea*) V & R

697. White-throated Rock-thrush (*Monticola gularis*) V
698. Chestnut-bellied Rock-thrush *(Monticola rufiventris)* V & R
699. Blue Rock-thrush (*Monticola solitarius*) V & R *
700. Blue Whistling-thrush *(Myophonus caeruleus)* R & V
701. Chestnut-capped Thrush (*Zoothera interpres*) R
702. Orange-headed Thrush (*Zoothera citrina*) R & V
703. Siberian Thrush (*Zoothera sibirica*) V
704. Long-tailed Thrush (*Zoothera dixoni*) V
705. Scaly Thrush (*Zoothera dauma*) R & V
706. Dark-sided Thrush (*Zoothera marginata*) R
707. Black-breasted Thrush (*Turdus dissimilis*) V
708. Grey-winged Blackbird (*Turdus boulboul*) V
709. Grey-sided Thrush (*Turdus feae*) V
710. Eye-browed Thrush *(Turdus obscurus)* V
711. Common Blackbird (*Turdus merula*) A
712. Chestnut Thrush (*Turdus rubrocanus*) V
713 a Red-throated Blackbird (*Turdus ruficollis ruficollis*) A
713 b Black-throated Thrush (*Turdus ruficollis atrogularis*) A
714. Dusky Thrush (*Turdus naumanni*) V
715. Japanese Thrush (*Turdus cardis*) A

Acanthizidae : **FLYEATER**
716. Flyeater (*Gerygone sulphurea*) R

Sylviidae : **OLD WORLD WARBLERS**
717. Lesser Whitethroat (*Sylvia curruca*) V
718. Golden-spectacled Warbler (*Seicercus burkii*) V
719. Grey-cheeked Warbler (*Seicercus poliogenys*) A
720. Chestnut-browed Warbler (*Seicercus castaniceps*) R
721. Yellow-bellied Warbler (*Abroscopus superciliaris*) R *
722. Rufous-faced Warbler (*Abroscopus albogularis*) R
723. Buff-throated Warbler (*Phylloscopus subaffinis*) V
724. Dusky Warbler (*Phylloscopus fuscatus*) V
725. Yellow-streaked Warbler (*Phylloscopus armandii*) V
726. Radde's Warbler (*Phylloscopus schwarzi*) V
727. Buff-barred Warbler *(Phylloscopus pulcher)* V
728. Inornate Warbler (*Phylloscopus inornatus*) V *

729. Lemon-rumped Warbler (*Phylloscopus proregulus*) V
730. Ashy-throated Warbler (*Phylloscopus maculipennis*) R
731. Arctic Warbler (*Phylloscopus borealis*) V
732. Greenish Warbler (*Phylloscopus trochiloides*) V
733. Two-barred Warbler (*Phylloscopus plumbeitarsus*) V
734. Pale-legged Leaf-Warbler (*Phylloscopus tenellipes*) V
735. Eastern-crowned Warbler (*Phylloscopus coronatus*) V
736. Blyth's Leaf-Warbler (*Phylloscopus reguloides*) V & R
737. White-tailed Leaf-Warbler (*Phylloscopus davisoni*) R
738. Yellow-vented Warbler (*Phylloscopus cantator*) V
739. Sulfur-breasted Warbler (*Phylloscopus ricketti*) V
740. Thick-billed Warbler (*Acrocephalus aedon*) V
741. Clamorous Reed-Warbler (*Acrocephalus stentoreus*) V
742. Great Reed-Warbler(*Acrocephalus arundinaceus*) V *
743. Black-browed Reed-Warbler (*Acrocephalus bistrigiceps*) V
744. Paddyfield Warbler (*Acrocephalus agricola*) V
745. Blunt-winged Warbler (*Acrocephalus concinens*) V
746. Pallas's Warbler (*Locustella certhiola*) V
747. Lanceolated Warbler (*Locustella lanceolata*) V
748. Striated Warbler (*Megalurus palustris*) R
749. Large Grass-Warbler (*Graminicola bengalensis*) E?
750. Common Tailorbird (*Orthotomus sutorius*) R *
751. Dark-necked Tailorbird (*Orthotomus atrogularis*) R *
752. Rufous-tailed Tailorbird (*Orthotomus sericeus*) R
753. Mountain Tailorbird (*Orthotomus cuculatus*) R
754. Ashy Tailorbird (*Orthotomus sepium*) R
755. Grey-breasted Prinia (*Prinia hodgsonii*) R
756. Rufescent Prinia (*Prinia rufescens*) R *
757. Tawny-flanked Prinia (*Prinia inornata*) R *
758. Yellow-bellied Prinia (*Prinia flaviventris*) R
759. Brown Prinia (*Prinia polychroa*) R
760. Hill Prinia (*Prinia atrogularis*) R

761. Zitting Cisticola (*Cisticola juncidis*) R
762. Bright-capped Cisticola (*Cisticola exilis*) R
763. Grey-bellied Tesia (*Tesia cyaniventer*) R
764. Slaty-bellied Tesia (*Tesia olivea*) R
765. Chestnut-headed Tesia (*Tesia castaneocoronata*) R
766. Stub-tailed Bush-Warbler (*Cettia squameiceps*) V
767. Pale-footed Bush-Warbler (*Cettia pallidipes*) R
768. Manchurian Bush-Warbler (*Cettia canturians*) V
769. Chestnut-crowned Bush-Warbler (*Cettia major*) A
770. Aberrant Bush-Warbler (*Cettia flavolivacea*) V
771. Chinese Bush-Warbler (*Bradypterus tacsanowskius*) A
772. Brown Bush-Warbler (*Bradypterus luteoventris*) V
773. Russet Bush-Warbler (*Bradypterus seebohmi*) R
774. Spotted Bush-Warbler (*Bradypterus thoracicus*) V

Muscicapidae : **FLYCATCHERS**
775. Fulvous-chested Flycatcher (*Rhinomyias olivacea*) R
776. Grey-chested Flycatcher (*Rhinomyias umbratilis*) R
777. Brown-chested Flycatcher (*Rhinomyias brunneata*) V
778. Dark-sided Flycatcher (*Muscicapa sibirica*) V
779. Asian Brown Flycatcher (*Muscicapa dauurica*) R & V
780. Brown-streaked Flycatcher (*Muscicapa williamsoni*) R & V
781. Ferruginous Flycatcher (*Muscicapa ferruginea*) V
782. Brown-breasted Flycatcher (*Muscicapa muttui*) R?
783. Yellow-rumped Flycatcher (*Ficedula zanthopygia*) V
784. Narcissus Flycatcher (*Ficedula narcissina*) V
785. Mugimaki Flycatcher (*Ficedula mugimaki*) V
786. Red-throated Flycatcher (*Ficedula parva*) V
787. Rufous-gorgetted Flycatcher (*Ficedula strophiata*) V
788. White-gorgetted Flycatcher (*Ficedula monileger*) R
789. Rufous-browed Flycatcher (*Ficedula solitaria*) R
790. Snowy-browed Flycatcher (*Ficedula hyperythra*) R
791. Rufous-chested Flycatcher (*Ficedula dumetoria*) R
792. Slaty-backed Flycatcher (*Ficedula hodgsonii*) V
793. Little Pied Flycatcher (*Ficedula westermanni*) R
794. Ultramarine Flycatcher (*Ficedula superciliaris*) V
795. Slaty-blue Flycatcher (*Ficedula tricolor*) V
796. Sapphire Flycatcher (*Ficedula sapphira*) V
797. Blue-and-white Flycatcher (*Cyanoptila cyanomelana*) V
798. Verditer Flycatcher (*Eumyias thalassina*) R & V
799. Large Niltava (*Niltava grandis*) R
800. Small Niltava (*Niltava macgrigoriae*) R
801. Fukien Niltava (*Niltava davidi*) V
802. Rufous-bellied Niltava (*Niltava sundara*) V
803. Vivid Niltava (*Niltava vivida*) V
804. White-tailed Flycatcher (*Cyornis concreta*) R
805. Hainan Blue Flycatcher (*Cyornis hainana*) R
806. Pale Blue Flycatcher (*Cyornis unicolor*) R
807. Blue-throated Flycatcher (*Cyornis rubeculoides*) R & V
808. Tickell's Blue Flycatcher (*Cyornis tickelliae*) R *
809. Mangrove Blue Flycatcher (*Cyornis rufigastra*) R
810. Malaysian Blue Flycatcher (*Cyornis turcosa*) R
811. Pygmy Blue Flycatcher (*Muscicapella hodgsoni*) V?
812. Grey-headed Flycatcher (*Culicicapa ceylonensis*) R & V *
813. Yellow-bellied Fantail (*Rhipidura hypoxantha*) R
814. White-throated Fantail (*Rhipidura albicollis*) R
815. White-browed Fantail (*Rhipidura aureola*) R
816. Spotted Fantail (*Rhipidura perlata*) R
817. Pied Fantail (*Rhipidura javanica*) R *
818 Black-naped Monarch (*Hypothymis azurea*) R *
819. Maroon-breasted Flycatcher (*Philentoma velatum*) R
820. Rufous-winged Flycatcher (*Philentoma pyrhopterum*) R
821. Japanese Paradise-Flycatcher (*Tersiphone atrocaudata*) V
822. Asian Paradise-Flycatcher (*Tersiphone paradisi*) R & V *

Pachycephalidae : **WHISTLERS**

823. Mangrove Whistler (*Pachycephala cinerea*) R

Motacillidae : **WAGTAILS, PIPITS**

824. White Wagtail (*Motacila alba*) V
825. Grey Wagtail (*Motacilla cinerea*) V *
826. Yellow Wagtail (*Motacilla flava*) V
827. Yellow-hooded Wagtail (*Motacilla citreola*) V
828. Forest Wagtail (*Dendronanthus indicus*) V
829. Olive Tree-Pipit (*Anthus hodgsoni*) V
830. Richard's Pipit (*Anthus novaeseelandiae* (R & V)
831. Red-throated Pipit (*Anthus cervinus*) V
832. Rosy Pipit (*Anthus roseatus*) V

Artamidae : **WOOD-SWALLOWS**

833. Ashy Wood-Swallow (*Artamus fuscus*) R *

Laniidae : **SHRIKES**

834. Brown Shrike (*Lanius cristatus*) V *
835. Tiger Shrike (*Lanius tigrinus*) V
836. Burmese Shrike (*Lanius collurioides*) R & V *
837. Long-tailed Shrike (*Lanius schach*) R *
838. Grey-backed Shrike (*Lanius rephronotus*) V

Sturnidae : **STARLINGS, MYNAS**

839. Philippine Glossy Starling (*Aplonis panayensis*) R
840. Spot-winged Starling (*Saraglossa spiloptera*) V
841. Common Starling (*Sturnus vulgaris*) V
842. Chestnut-tailed Starling (*Sturnus malabaricus*) R & V
843. White-shouldered Starling (*Sturnus sinensis*) V
844. Purple-backed Starling (*Sturnus sturninus*) V
845. Brahminy Starling (*Sturnus pagodarum*) A
846. Rosy Starling (*Sturnus roseus*) A
847. Asian Pied Starling (*Sturnus contra*) R *
848. Black-collared Starling (*Sturnus nigricollis*) R *
849. Vinous-breasted Starling (*Sturnus burmannicus*) R
850. Common Myna (*Acridotheres tristis*) R *
851. White-vented Myna (*Acridotheres javanicus*) R *
852. Jungle Myna (*Acridotheres fuscus*) R *
853. Golden-crested Myna (*Ampeliceps coronatus*) R
854. Hill Myna (*Gracula religiosa*) R *

Nectariniidae : **SUNBIRDS,**

SPIDERHUNTERS

855. Plain Sunbird (*Anthreptes simplex*) R
856. Brown-throated Sunbird (*Anthreptes malacensis*) R
857. Red-throated Sunbird (*Anthreptes rhodolaema*) R
858. Ruby-cheeked Sunbird (*Anthreptes singalensis*) R
859. Purple-naped Sunbird (*Hypogramma hypogrammicum*) R
860. Purple-throated Sunbird (*Nectarinia sperata*) R
861. Copper-throated Sunbird (*Nectarinia calcostetha*) R
862. Olive-backed Sunbird (*Nectarinia jugularis*) R
863. Purple Sunbird (*Nectarinia asiatica*) R
864. Gould's Sunbird (*Aethopyga gouldiae*) V
865. Green-tailed Sunbird (*Aethopyga nipalensis*) R
866. Black-throated Sunbird (*Aethopyga saturata*) R
867. Crimson Sunbird (*Aethopyga siparaja*) R
868. Fire-tailed Sunbird (*Aethopyga ignicauda*) A
869. Scarlet Sunbird (*Aethopyga temminckii*) R
870. Little Spiderhunter (*Arachnothera longirostra*) R
871. Thick-billed Spiderhunter (*Arachnothera crassirostris*)R
872. Long-billed Spiderhunter (*Arachnothera robusta*) R
873. Spectacled Spiderhunter (*Arachnothera flavigaster*) R
874. Yellow-eared Spiderhunter (*Arachnothera chrysogenys*) R
875. Grey-breasted Spiderhunter (*Arachnothera affinis*) R
876. Streaked Spiderhunter (*Arachnothera magna*) R

Dicaeidae : **FLOWERPECKERS**

877. Scarlet-breasted Flowerpecker (*Prionochilus thoracicus*) R
878. Yellow-breasted Flowerpecker (*Prionochilus maculatus*) R
879. Crimson-breasted Flowerpecker (*Prionochilus percussus*) R
880. Thick-billed Flowerpecker (*Dicaeum agile*) R
881. Yellow-vented Flowerpecker (*Dicaeum chrysorrheum*) R
882. Yellow-bellied Flowerpecker (*Dicaeum melanoxanthum*) R?
883. Orange-bellied Flowerpecker (*Dicaeum trigonostigma*) R

884. Plain Flowerpecker (*Dicaeum concolor*) R
885. Scarlet-backed Flowerpecker (*Dicaeum cruentatum*) R *
886. Buff-bellied Flowerpecker (*Dicaeum ignipectus*) R

Zosteropidae : WHITE-EYES
887. Chestnut-flanked White-Eye (*Zosterops erythropleura*) V
888. Japanese White-Eye (*Zosterops japonica*) V
889. Oriental Palpebrosa (*Zosterops palpebrosa*) R *
890. Everett's White-Eye (*Zosterops everetti*) R

Ploceidae : SPARROWS, WEAVERS, MUNIAS
891. Eurasian Tree Sparrow (*Passer montanus*) R *
892. House Sparrow (*Passer domesticus*) R *
893. Plain-backed Sparrow (*Passer flaveolus*) R *
894. Russet Sparrow (*Passer rutilans*) V
895. Baya Weaver (*Ploceus philippinus*) R *
896. Streaked Weaver (*Ploceus manyar*) R
897. Asian Golden Weaver (*Ploceus hypoxanthus*) R *
898. Red Avadavat (*Amandava amandava*) R
899. Pin-tailed Parrotfinch (*Erythrura prasina*) R
900. Java Sparrow (*Padda oryzivora*) R
901. White-rumped Munia (*Lonchura striata*) R *
902. White-bellied Munia (*Lonchura leucogastra*) R
903. Scaly-breasted Munia (*Lonchura punctulata*) R *
904. Chestnut Munia (*Lonchura malacca*) R
905. White-headed Munia (*Lonchura maja*) R

Fringillidae : FINCHES
906. Black-headed Greenfinch (*Carduelis ambigua*) V
907. Dark-breasted Rosefinch (*Carpodacus nipalensis*) V
908. CommonRosefinch (*Carpodacus erythrinus*) V
909. Pink-rumped Rosefinch (*Carpodacus eos*) A
910. Brambling (*Fringilla montifringilla*) A
911. Scarlet Finch (*Haematospiza sipahi*) V
912. Spot-winged Grosbeak (*Mycerobas melanozanthos*) R
913. Collared Grosbeak (*Mycerobas affinis*) A
914. Yellow-billed Grosbeak (*Eophona migratoria*) A

Emberizidae : BUNTINGS
915. Tristram's Bunting (*Emberiza tristrami*) A
916. Chestnut-eared Bunting (*Emberiza fucata*) V
917. Little Bunting (*Emberiza pusilla*) V
918. Yellow-breasted Bunting (*Emberiza aureola*) V
919. Black-headed Bunting (*Emberiza melanocephala*) A
920. Chestnut Bunting (*Emberiza rutila*) V
921. Black-faced Bunting (*Emberiza spodocephala*) V
922. Crested Bunting (*Melophus lathami*) V *

175

Index

176

178